S0-BDO-498

The Making of

a Man of God –

Studies in

I and II Timothy

Dean Fetterhoff

BMH Books

Winona Lake, Indiana

ISBN: 0-88469-030-X

COPYRIGHT 1976
BMH BOOKS
WINONA LAKE, INDIANA

Printed in U.S.A.

Cover Design: Tim Kennedy

Acknowledgments

The author desires to express his gratitude to Rev. Ivan French, instructor in Theology and Church History, Grace Theological Seminary, Winona Lake, Indiana, who took valuable time from a busy schedule to read the manuscript and write the foreword to this book.

Grateful appreciation is also expressed to the following ladies of the Grace Brethren Church of Greater Atlanta, Georgia, for their assistance in typing the manuscript: Audrey Batroff, Dorothy Bustraan, Shirley Duckwitz, Patricia Hicks, Barbara McPheeters, Linda Ross and Phyllis Williams.

DEDICATION

Just as there were two women in the life of Timothy whose influence was foundational in the making of this man of God (II Tim. 1:5); so there have been two women in my life whose example of faith, whose prayers, and whose encouragement have contributed more than any others toward making me a "man of God." Therefore, this book is lovingly dedicated to

my beloved wife,

BILLIE,

and

my mother,

MRS. BEULAH FETTERHOFF

Foreword

The Pastoral Epistles deal with preachers and people. Here are directions, exhortations and warnings to the people who make up the church of God and to the leaders who have the heavy responsibility of the ministry of the church.

All who read the pages of *The Making of a Man of God* will be aware that the author knows the church—both as it ought to be according to the scriptural pattern and as it actually is with all of its weaknesses and shortcomings.

The wide experience of Dean Fetterhoff has uniquely equipped him for the task of guiding others through a study of these two New Testament books. He has been a full-time evangelist, a successful soul winner and educator and now is the pastor of a thriving, growing church. The wisdom gained from years of varied experiences and the warmth of his love and concern for people is easily detected in this helpful study manual of First and Second Timothy. Here is guidance for servants and saints. Here is a happy combination of principle and practice spelled out in a most useful manner.

I am happy to commend this study manual to all who are a part of "the church of the living God, the pillar and ground of the truth" (I Tim. 3:15).

Ivan H. French
Grace Theological Seminary

Introduction

Timothy—The Young Preacher

The apostle Paul experienced persecution and suffering for the sake of the Lord Jesus as have few men in history (cf. II Cor. 11:24-33). During some of those dark hours of suffering one of the sources of comfort and encouragement must have been when he thought of the young preacher, Timothy. "Timothy has been worth it all," he may have said, "there's nobody else like him" (cf. Phil. 2:20). Not only was Paul strengthened because of Timothy's faithfulness in service for Christ, but that which immensely added to Paul's joy was that Timothy was his "own son in the faith." Every winner of souls echoes the words of John, "I have no greater joy than to hear that my children walk in truth" (III John 4), and Timothy brought that joy to Paul's heart.

The son of a Greek father, who likely was an unbeliever, and a godly Jewish mother and grandmother (Acts 16:1, 3 and II Tim. 1:5), Timothy was probably won to Christ by the apostle Paul on his first missionary journey. Paul preached at Lystra on this tour, and Timothy was a native of this city (Acts 14:6-23). Perhaps Timothy had been a witness to the miracle of the healing of the cripple of Lystra which led to the worship of Paul and Barnabas by the townspeople and the priest of Jupiter. When Paul and Barnabas rejected this worship and exhorted the people to turn to the living God, the mob completely reversed its attitude and stoned Paul, leaving him for dead. At what point Timothy yielded his heart to Christ we don't know, but somewhere along the line in hearing Paul's message and seeing his suffering the young man bowed his knee to Paul's Lord and was saved. We do not know whether or not Paul knew of Timothy's conversion at that time. There is no record of anyone else receiving the Saviour on this occasion at Lystra (with the possible exception of the lame man who was healed and the fact that "disciples" are mentioned in Acts 14:20). But out of the birth pangs of near physical death the apostle Paul brought forth the one who may have been the oustanding convert of his entire ministry—Timothy.

When Paul came to Lystra on his second missionary journey, Timothy had grown spiritually into a young disciple with a fine spiritual reputation. He was evidently of such unusual character and spiritual dedication that Paul recognized him as one he would like to have join his evangelistic party. This was the beginning of a relationship that was to last possibly until the martyrdom of the great apostle in the city of Rome.

Trying to trace the ministry of Timothy and his journeys with Paul is no easy task! This is not because the Biblical information is incorrect but because it does not fill in the details of all the journeys and ministry of Paul. Such matters as whether Paul experienced one Roman imprisonment or two have a great deal to do with the journeys of Timothy and the writing of the epistles which bear his name. Several different itineraries may be argued, but none may be proved conclusively. However, we may follow Timothy's ministry with a general degree of accuracy for the most part.

Paul first circumcised Timothy, not that he might be more accepted among fellow Christians but for his acceptance with the Jews who knew his father was a Greek. From Lystra Timothy accompanied Paul on his journey, but nothing further is said about him until they had traveled at least four hundred miles and had ministered in Philippi and Thessalonica and arrived at Berea. When Paul left Berea to go to Athens, Timothy and Silas stayed behind (Acts 17:14). Before leaving, Paul may have instructed them to return to Thessalonica and this may be the time that the visit recorded in I Thessalonians 3:2 and 6 was made. After Paul arrived in Athens, he sent word for Timothy and Silas to join him as soon as possible (Acts 17:15), but they did not arrive until Paul was in Corinth (Acts 18:5). Paul continued in Corinth a year and six months, apparently along with Silas and Timothy. He returned to Antioch after some time and it is not stated whether Timothy accompanied him or not. Nothing more is heard from Timothy until Paul returned to Ephesus at the beginning of his third and last missionary journey. Dr. Merrill Unger states that five years had elapsed since Paul's last appearance. At this time Paul sent Timothy and Erastus into Macedonia (Acts 19:22) which included a trip to Corinth (I Cor. 4:17; 16:10). Paul then left Ephesus and journeyed throughout Macedonia on a preaching mission and came into Greece, where he stayed three months (Acts 20:1-3). Timothy and several others now preceded Paul as he began to retrace his steps and again came to Troas (Acts 20:5).

Nothing further is said about Timothy in the Book of Acts, but we know he was with Paul when he was in prison in Rome (see opening verses of Philippians, Colossians and Philemon). It may have been that Timothy accompanied Paul during his trip to Jerusalem, arrest, imprisonment and journey to Rome. The Book of Hebrews states that Timothy, himself, was imprisoned and then set free (13:23). In Paul's last epistle, II Timothy, he asks that Timothy come as quickly as possible and bring certain items with him that Paul had left at Troas (II Tim. 4:9,13,21). If he arrived before Paul's martyrdom, Timothy may have witnessed that shameful deed.

The Book of I Timothy

This author accepts the fact that I Timothy was written, as stated in the opening verses, by the beloved father-in-the-faith and long-traveling companion of Timothy, the apostle Paul. Although the Word of God is capable of the minute examination of critical scholarship and has stood the tests of such scholarship through the decades of time, this author becomes weary of the destructively critical and sometimes blasphemous attacks which are made upon nearly every portion of the Word of God. To be skeptical, cynical and blasphemous are not necessarily marks of intellectualism, although in some circles they seem to be equated with such. I Timothy has not escaped this criticism. However, objections have been raised concerning the genuineness (who wrote it) and authenticity (whether or not it tells the truth) of the book, and these problems have been resolved by men equally as scholarly as those who raised them. It is not the purpose of this author to go into detail in these matters, but the reader is referred to Dr. Homer Kent, Jr.,'s fine work on *The Pastoral Epistles* (pp. 24-71) where these problems are discussed. We proceed on the basis that Paul wrote both epistles to Timothy and that we have those two epistles in our Bible.

The time of the writing of I Timothy revolves around whether Paul experienced one or two imprisonments at Rome. We know that the epistle was written after Paul left Ephesus and went into Macedonia (I Tim. 1:3). There is only one such incident recorded in the Book of Acts (Acts 20:1). Paul had previously sent Timothy into Macedonia and later Timothy is said to have preceded Paul to Troas, which is also in Macedonia (20:14). If Paul wrote I Timothy after his departure from Ephesus, Timothy must have returned to Ephesus from Macedonia before Paul left. He could have stayed there after Paul left long enough to receive the epistle from him and to carry out the instructions in the epistle and yet leave and precede Paul to Troas. I think this is highly unlikely although Albert Barnes and other scholars hold this position. This would put the writing around A.D. 58.

The view more widely held by conservative scholarship is that Paul was freed from his first imprisonment in Rome and that he traveled throughout the East, including a trip to Macedonia. This seems likely in view of the fact that there is nothing in I Timothy to indicate that Christianity had been outlawed by the Roman government (as it was at the writing of II Timothy). In this case, Paul wrote I Timothy following his release in A.D. 62, which would place the date of the writing at A.D. 63 or 64. Christianity was then declared illegal and Paul was again imprisoned at which time II Timothy was written.

Why Study These Books?

When I ask why we should study these books, you may answer in a bit of shock and surprise, "Why? Because they are in the Bible!" Good! I like that kind of loyalty and faith in the Scriptures. However, every portion of the Word of God has its unique purpose and message for us. What is the purpose and message of these books? William Hendriksen in his commentary on the Pastoral Epistles suggests several reasons, and I would like to repeat some of them here.

1. Because they stress *sound doctrine.* A popular philosophy says: "It doesn't make any difference what you believe as long as you are sincere." You won't find that kind of philosophy in Paul's writing to Timothy! It makes all the difference in the world and your eternity depends on what you believe. We'd better be sure that what we believe corresponds to what God has said!

2. Because they demand *consecrated living.* Paul's exhortation to Timothy to be an example of the believer, the qualifications for bishops and deacons, and the admonition to modesty given to women all have to do with "practical theology"—sound doctrine demonstrated in a godly life.

3. Because these epistles give much-needed advice and direction in proper *church administration.* These instructions given here are foundational for church organization and are just as relevant in the 20th century as they were in the day they were given. A lot of church problems would be avoided or eliminated by adhering to the guidance given in these books.

4. Because they shed *additional light on the closing years of the great life of the apostle Paul.* The Book of Acts closes leaving us wondering what happened to Paul after his trip to Rome as a prisoner and the brief description of his imprisonment there. The Holy Spirit saw fit to continue the story of his life through these epistles. Other reasons are given by Harrison

and many more could be added. Any one of these reasons would be sufficient to warrant a careful study of these epistles, but taken together they should cause us to be eager to want to know what God has to say to us through these inspired writings.

Paul's epistles to Timothy have been a source of guidance and encouragement for every man who seeks to minister the Word of God. Although these, along with the epistle to Titus, have been called the Pastoral Epistles, Timothy is not to be thought of in the same capacity as a modern-day pastor. The church at Ephesus already had elders who were in charge of the work there (Acts 19:17-38). Timothy was rather Paul's personal representative to give direction and instruction not only to Ephesus but to all the churches throughout that area—guarding against false doctrine and giving instruction for church organization. Thus the letters have been included in the eternal Word of God as instruction to local churches and pastors of all time, and probably no other epistles of the New Testament have been so valuable in these areas. May they prove so in this study, whether the readers are pastors of churches or those children of God in local assemblies who are seeking to be perfected "for the work of the ministry" (Eph. 4:12).

Just a word about the nature of this book before we move on to a more minute study of it. Although I have endeavored to give careful attention to a technical and critical study of these epistles, this book is not written from that standpoint. It is written in popular style with the purpose and goal in mind of causing the reader to be interested, challenged and excited about this study. The lay people have been primarily in mind in the writing, as well as the critical scholar. This book is in no sense to be used as a substitute for studying the two epistles themselves. It is only intended as a guide to their study. If the reader is caused to become excited about new spiritual truth which he never saw before, to love the Lord Jesus Christ more, and to desire to serve Him better as a result of the study, then the effort required to write it will have been time well spent. God grant that it may be so.

Table of

Contents

The Making

of a

Man of God –

Studies in

I and II Timothy

1

Doctrine Is Important

I Timothy 1:1-11

THE CHAPTER OUTLINED:

I. **The Greeting**

II. **The Responsibility to Maintain Sound Doctrine**
   A. The warning against false doctrine
   B. The product of sound doctrine
   C. The forsaking of sound doctrine

III. **The Background of Sound Doctrine**
   A. The goodness of the law
   B. Those free from the law
   C. Those bound by the law

A pastor once asked me to hold an evangelistic meeting for him. He qualified his invitation by saying: "I want you to come and preach the Gospel, but I don't want you to preach doctrine." A difficult request indeed! The word "doctrine" as used in the New Testament means "teaching." Now although I have heard some sermons that went on for a half hour or more and never did teach much of anything, I seriously doubt if this man wanted that. He was afraid I might jump on some particular "denominational doctrine" instead of preaching the Gospel. However, he was wrong in his terminology. Doctrine encompasses everything we believe. Therefore, doctrine is important! We shall see that Paul emphasizes this fact in this epistle. Before we do so, however, let us take note of the short introduction to the letter.

I. THE GREETING (vv. 1-2).

As was the custom of the day, the writer opened the letter with his signature—Paul. Perhaps this custom should be practiced today. Have you ever received a letter with no name or return address on the outside? I dare say the first thing you did was to look at the end of the letter to see who wrote it.

This was not to be a mere friendly, informal letter to friend Timothy. Paul officially identifies himself as "an apostle of Jesus Christ." Timothy knew that, but this letter was to have wide circulation and importance. The word "apostle" simply means "one sent." Of Paul and the twelve it is used as an official title, and he uses it here to establish an official relationship.

Paul gives further weight to his calling by emphasizing that his appointment as an apostle was not of his own doing. In nearly every epistle he emphasizes this appointment was "by the will of God." Here he says it is "by the commandment of God our Saviour, and Lord Jesus Christ, which is our hope." This was equal to an official statement of the day, the same as saying "by order of." Paul knew he was called to this position by almighty God and he did not take that calling lightly. May it be so with every child of God, no matter how lofty or lowly that calling may be. There are no unimportant officers in the army of God.

The recipient of the letter was one of Paul's own converts, his traveling companion and perhaps his dearest friend. Although this was to be an official letter, Paul speaks of Timothy with genuine tenderness.

Paul's greeting is noteworthy—"Grace, mercy, and peace." Have you ever noticed that these three words are always in this order in the greetings of the New Testament? It must be so. No man can have peace until first of all he has experienced the grace and mercy of God. Mercy follows grace because it is based on the grace of God. We deserve no mercy and find no peace apart from God's grace. Oh, that the statesmen who seek world peace and individuals who search for personal peace might learn this!

II. THE RESPONSIBILITY TO MAINTAIN SOUND DOCTRINE (vv. 3-7).

A. The warning against false doctrine (vv. 3-4).

One of the prime purposes for which Paul wanted Timothy to stay in Ephesus was to counteract the teaching of those who were teaching "other doctrine." These individuals are not named (as are Hymenaeus and Alexander of v. 20), but are simply referred to as "certain individuals." This is probably not because Paul did not know who they were, but because he didn't want to give them status by including their names in this official letter. Timothy is to warn them that they are "not to teach other doctrine" (lit. Greek trans.). The expression used here is important. There are two Greek words used for "other" in the New Testament. One, *alla,* means "another of the same kind." The second is *heteros* which means "a different kind." It is the second word that is used here. This doctrine was different from anything Paul had ever taught. These words are used in Galatians 1:6-7 where the Galatians were accused of preaching a gospel which was "not another" (v. 7—*alla,* the same kind), but was "another" (v. 6—*heteros,* a different kind). Timothy was to "charge" these men to stop it! In teaching a different doctrine they were striking at the very heart of the Christian faith. Fidelity to the doctrine of the Word of God is not optional for the child of God.

This "different doctrine" didn't bring sinners to salvation or edify the believers. It only resulted in curiosity and their pursuing myths ("fables") and "endless geneologies." The Jews have been guilty of allegorizing much of the Old Testament, of adding stories, of taking some of the geneological tables of the Old Testament and adding names with symbolic meanings. Whole tales were woven about them. People don't change a bit! How many false cults and heresies have been started in our day by exactly the same means. People are fascinated by some new, wild symbolism (everything from the "spiritual" measurements of the pyramids to naming a current world figure the Antichrist on the basis of the number of letters in his name, and so on) and yet remain ignorant of the Gospel of the saving grace of God.

All such fleshly meanderings only lead to more and more questions and involvement. They suck the person in like a whirlpool. They do not result in the "stewardship of God" (better translation than "godly edifying"). Paul says that we have been made stewards of the mysteries of God, and we are required to be found faithful to that stewardship (I Cor. 4:1-2). The "different doctrine" in Ephesus and the curious allegorizing of the Bible today don't measure up!

B. The product of sound doctrine (v. 5).

Paul now shows what sound doctrine will produce. When he speaks of "the end of the commandment," he is not talking about the Ten Commandments. The Greek word here is not *entole* (used when referring to the Ten Commandments) but *paraggelia*, the same word as "charge" in verse 3. The "end" here is the goal. Here is the destination toward which the Word of God is preached and taught. The following three things will result.

1. "Love out of a pure heart." There are three Greek words for love. *Eros* has to do with sensual passion, sexual involvement. Our word "erotic" is from this. This word is not used in the New Testament. The second word is *phileo*, meaning "affection, human feeling or tenderness." We live in a society which can't seem to tell the difference between these two and can't seem to move from the first to the second. The third Greek word for love is *agapao* and refers to divine love, love which is measured by sacrifice. It is the love of John 3:16. This is the word which is used here. Sound doctrine produces God's love in our hearts. This love comes from a "pure" heart, a heart that has been cleansed and made pure by the blood of Christ.

2. The second product of sound doctrine is "a good conscience." "Let your conscience be your guide." Ever hear that? This is the rule of life for many, and some are probably basing their hope of heaven on it. Good advice—right? Not necessarily and not always. You see, your conscience can be influenced. Your conscience acts on the basis of the knowledge it has. In India in the past there were mothers who threw their babies into the Ganges River. Their consciences would have hurt them it they had not done it. However, their consciences were wrong! They had been fed the wrong information. A "good conscience" is one which has been "purged" by the blood of Christ from dead works (Heb. 9:14) and is now serving the living God. It now gives guidance to the individual based upon the information it has in the light of the Word of God as applied by the Holy Spirit.

3. The final product of sound doctrine listed here is "faith unfeigned."

The adjective used to describe faith which is the result of sound doctrine is *anupokritos*. Pronounce it out loud—*anupokritos*, "unhypocritical" faith. How much the testimony of Christ has been hurt because of people who professed a faith they did not possess. Their lives have denied what their lips professed. In contrast, when the sinner genuinely comes to Christ and believes the "sound doctrine" of the Scriptures, he no longer has to "play act" at being a Christian. He now has an "unhypocritical" faith.

C. The forsaking of sound doctrine (vv. 6-7).

These self-appointed teachers of verse 3 who were teaching "other doctrine" have swerved, completely missing the mark when it comes to sound teaching. Paul says they have "turned aside." This is a medical term which means "to turn or twist." Have you ever seriously "turned" your ankle? This wasn't something you laughed about and then went skipping merrily on your way! It may have caused excruciating pain, brought tears to your eyes and perhaps even put you on crutches for a while. This is what these false teachers were doing to the body of Christ. This was no mere trifling in splitting theological hairs. It was a serious departure from sound doctrine. The result was "vain jangling," a lot of words that didn't say anything or lead anywhere. How many times I have listened to the empty oratory of some liberal preacher who, as Vance Havner says, practiced "the art of almost saying something."

These teachers who had infiltrated the church at Ephesus professed to be specialists. They were "law-teachers," ones claiming to be experts in the Old Testament law. Although these men presented themselves as great authorities, they didn't really know what they were talking about. Their teaching led in circles and went nowhere, but what they stated they did so with great force and confidence. As Vincent says, "They know not *what* they say, nor what kind of things they are *of which* they speak so confidently. The false teachers announce their errors with assurance." This reminds us of the preacher's sermon notes which had penciled on the side, "Weak here. Shout!" Just because a man pounds the pulpit, shouts and goes through all sorts of gymnastics when preaching doesn't mean he is saying much or preaching the truth. It's doctrine that counts!

III. THE BACKGROUND OF SOUND DOCTRINE (vv. 8-11).

A. The goodness of the law (v. 8).

Lest Paul be misunderstood, he now makes it clear that he is not speaking against the law itself, but against those who are using the law improperly. Paul emphasizes the intrinsic goodness of the law again in Romans 7:7,12–"What shall we say then? Is the law sin? God forbid. ... Wherefore the law is holy, and the commandment holy, and just, and good." One can discern throughout much of the New Testament that there were those who would seek to dilute the doctrine of salvation by grace by making the law a part of salvation or a rule of life for the Christian (see Romans and Galatians et al). Human nature seems to want to "do something" to merit salvation. This is true whether it be Jewish law-keeping in Paul's day or whether it be the salvation-by-works of the cults and liberalism of today. God will have none of this. Salvation is by the grace of God alone, based upon the sacrifice of His Son on Calvary– this plus nothing.

B. Those free from the law (v. 9).

Paul now turns to the proper use of the law and its purpose. Law is made for unrighteous men. Several months ago I was conducting an evangelistic meeting in a midwestern city and was invited to speak at the noonday chapel service of an industrial plant. The ownership and management of the plant were Christian men, and they had instituted a chapel service as a part of the lunch-hour program. This particular plant was engaged in the manufacturing of locks. After the service I went on a tour of the plant. I was fascinated by the intricate engineering and many details that went into the making of padlocks. Many, many varieties were being manufactured for specific use by the different clients—some were for shops and businesses, some for private homes, some for penal institutions, some for the navy, and so on and so forth. As I toured the plant, all of a sudden the thought came to me: "This plant is thriving on the dishonesty of man! If there were no law-breakers, this plant would be out of business!" If all men were good men, there would need be no locks on doors, either to keep men in or out. We can scarcely imagine how much our society would change if this were true. Sad to say, such is definitely not the case. We need laws, perhaps today more than ever before. Yes, the law was not made for righteous men but for unrighteous.

C. Those bound by the law (vv. 9-10).

A list now follows illustrating those to whom the law applies and for whom it was made. It is interesting that the list falls into two categories, sins against God (through "profane") and sins against man (through "perjured persons"). This would lead us to believe that Paul is referring to the Mosaic Law because the Ten Commandments fall naturally into the same two divisions.

Paul first speaks of those who are "lawless and disobedient." To us this seems to be saying the same thing. However, this is not the case. The first has to do with recognizing no law. Those who rebel at all constituted authority. This is the same word which is used in Matthew 24:12 where we are told that one of the characteristics of the last days is that "iniquity [lawlessness] shall abound." These days in which men freely flaunt the law serve to illustrate the truth that law and its enforcement are needed as never before. The second word, "disobedient," has not so much to do with not recognizing the law or breaking it, but a general attitude of failure to bring oneself under subjection to anyone or anything. "Do your own thing." Ever hear that? While it may well mean that the individual should not try to present a false front in being something that he is not, it usually demonstrates a rebellion and lack of subordination to anyone or anything. Every man is a law unto himself. We seem to live in a time much like that described during the days of the judges in Israel—"every man did that which was right in his own eyes" (Judges 21:25). Those here described recognize no legal obligation, and subjection to any law is refused. For these the law was made and to them it applies, like it or not.

This is followed by those who are described as "ungodly" and "sinners." In the first term Paul is describing an attitude toward God. It means "destitute of reverential awe toward God, impious." God doesn't make any real difference in the life. He is not seen as the holy and righteous Being of eternity. He is thought of only as "the man upstairs," or the "somebody" who "up there likes me." This attitude can be readily seen in the lives of men today and in society in general. Although men would probably not outrightly deny the existence of God, their lives demonstrate that there is a practical atheism about them which does not consider God relevant or important. These are "ungodly."

Whereas "ungodly" gives the negative description of men (a general attitude of impiety toward God), "sinners" describes the positive action of life. This is the word commonly used for sin in the New Testament and refers to "missing the mark." It would include not only those who live wickedly and whom even unregenerate society would recognize as "sinners" but also those who are "good" in the eyes of others, those who are religious. Paul includes himself in this group in verse 15 and actually says he was the worst of the whole group, even though he was unsurpassed in dedication to his religion (Phil. 3:4-6).

The word "unholy" is similar in its meaning to "ungodly" which was previously used and has the idea of impiety toward God. Because God doesn't have any real place of importance in the lives of men, those lives are not characterized by holiness or piety. It is interesting that the term "unholy" seems to correspond in the mind of Paul to "Remember the sabbath day, to keep it holy." In recent years we have seen an illustration of this in society in relation to the observance of Sunday as a day of rest and worship. Several years ago the writer recalls a great controversy which took place in the city in which he was living because July 4th fell on Sunday that year. And even though the city and nation was observing Monday as a legal holiday a big parade and fireworks display had been planned for the Lord's day. Those who planned the affair admitted that it had just not occurred to them that there would be a problem by scheduling the event on Sunday. Of course not! Men in whose lives God has no practical place will not give Him much consideration in their actions. However, the real problem is that men who do not "like to retain God in their knowledge" (Rom. 1:28) have no desire to set aside one day per week to worship Him. I would carefully point out that it is true that the Christian is no longer bound by the law to worship on the Sabbath. In fact, we are not to have one day as a sacred day (Col. 2:16) with other days considered secular. Every day is sacred for the Christian! However, we gather on the Lord's Day to worship our Lord and to commemorate the resurrection of the Saviour, and I for one want to do all I can to preserve that practice.

Next is the word "profane." The background and meaning of this word is interesting. The Greek word means "accessible, lawful, to be trodden." The idea can be more clearly seen from the meaning of our English word, meaning "before" (pro) and "temple" (fane), thus that which is in front of the temple and may be walked upon. As used here it has the idea of trampling on that which is holy. The man who has no real conception of the holiness, righteousness and glory of God will not consider God in his actions and things which are holy will be to him as something that may be walked all over and treated with disregard.

I would add that although swearing or profanity as we know it is not specifically referred to here, it is certainly included in the larger meaning of the term. As the hearts of men have no place for God and there is no fear of Him before their eyes (Rom. 3:18), this attitude will spill out their mouths. This seems evident today as never before. Not only do men blaspheme and curse the God of heaven, but people who would profess to be religious and even claim to believe in and worship God think nothing of profaning the name of God. How often do we hear men say, "My God," or "O God" concerning trivial matters in the course of their conversation. Usually they are hardly aware they have said it. Such expressions ought not to fall from the lips of a Christian, and they ought to grieve our hearts when we hear them from others.

Paul now turns to sins against mankind and the parallel with the Decalogue becomes even more evident. The word used for "murderers" of fathers and mothers is not the same as "manslayers" in the last part of the verse. Although it includes killing, it is a broader word, really better translated "smiter" and can include any unnatural treatment of parents. Many a mother and father have been all but "killed" by the ingratitude and sin of wayward sons and daughters.

It is interesting to note that actual killing of parents was so unthinkable in Roman times that there was no law made for punishment of such crimes. As we think of the decadence of Roman society, we are made to wonder if our society has not surpassed it in moral decay, for the killing of parents is certainly not unheard of today. On the same day these words were being written, the author heard a local news report that told how a daughter had killed her mother by taking an axe and hacking her skull in two! We are reminded of Paul's words in II Timothy which speak of the last days. "Without natural affection" (3:3) is one of the marks of the conclusion of this age of grace. Natural love would certainly prohibit such a crime as is here named, but perhaps as this age nears its end even the sin of murder of parents will not be uncommon.

"Manslayers" does not refer to accidental death such as does the word "manslaughter" which we use today. This is the only place in the New Testament where this word is used and there is no question but that Paul is talking about murder—homicide. This is a crime which God says is to be punished by death (Gen. 9:6). God's command for the crime of murder is capital punishment, and this has never been abrogated. Several years ago there were those who argued that statistics showed that capital punishment was no deterrent to homicide and that capital punishment violated the rights of the offender, and so forth. It was finally decided that capital punishment was "cruel and unusual punishment" and it was declared unconstitutional. (I wonder if God considered that when He gave the command of Gen. 9:6!) Somehow the statistics have been forgotten as we have seen homicides skyrocket since the abolishment of capital punishment. Today the public is clamoring for the reinstatement of the punishment. Maybe God knew best after all!

The apostle then turns to sex sins. "Whoremongers" is the word which is usually translated "fornicators." It has been argued that fornication in the Bible refers primarily to sexual sin prior to marriage and adultery refers to the same sin after marriage. While this distinction may be observed in some places, fornication includes marital infidelity in other passages. This seems to be indicated here since Paul is following the Ten Commandments in listing sins in this passage and this corresponds to "Thou shalt not commit adultery." Let it be further pointed out, however, that the Greek word originally referred to sexual intercourse before marriage. This should make perfectly clear, along with many other passages and principles taught in the Word, that the Bible expressly forbids premarital sex. It is sad that this comment needs to be made, but it is necessary because this has become accepted as a way of life among unregenerate society. It is sin and cannot be rationalized as anything else!

Paul then turns from immorality between the sexes to that which may be considered on the bottom rung of the ladder of sex sins—sodomy, "them that defile themselves with mankind." We live in a day when every form of sin seems to find some justification. It is not surprising, therefore, that the sin mentioned here is looked upon as an accepted way of life and those involved as "normal" citizens of society. We hear of homosexual churches, homosexual ministers, and even homosexual wedding ceremonies in which the blessing of God is blasphemously called upon those formally united in this sin. It is indeed alarming how men can flagrantly violate the Word of God in the name of God!

Paul continues his list of sins in correspondence to the Ten Commandments by mentioning the worst kind of violation of the commandment, "Thou shalt not steal." This is the "menstealing," or as we say today, "kidnapping." This is certainly timely in view of the wave of political kidnapping which has swept over the world today. Did you know that in Argentina bank robbing has almost ceased, because there is a way to get money that is far less risky and involves much more money—kidnapping? We are told that over 500 kidnappings took place in one year in that country. It is also interesting to note that the word "menstealers" comes from the word meaning "slavery" and therefore probably refers primarily to slave-dealers. How much suffering and grief has come to this world as a result of slavery, not only in the lives of those who are stolen as slaves but in the nations where slavery either is or has been practiced. USA . . . illustration number one!

"Liars . . . perjured persons" complete the list of sins specifically named. Lying is an accepted way of life in much of the world. Missionaries tell us that they simply adjust their thinking to compensate for what a man may say, knowing full well that he is lying. This becomes a very serious problem to be reckoned with in many cases when the unbeliever in such a society is converted. In our own nation, shading the truth, finding loopholes for tax evasion, and leaving the wrong impression are all practiced without pangs of conscience by many who refuse to face these and similar matters for just what they really are—lying.

Every other offense to God can be included under the umbrella of "any other thing that is contrary to sound doctrine." This evidently corresponds to "Thou shalt not covet" in Paul's parallel with the Decalogue. Covetousness rises out of a heart which is full of pride and centered on self. This pride and self-centeredness is perhaps the basis of all sin. It is interesting that Paul did not say "anything that is contrary to sound action," but rather contrary to sound "doctrine." What a person believes determines how he lives.

D. The basis of sound doctrine—the Gospel (v. 11).

The Gospel had been perverted and diluted by those "teachers of the law" who evoked the problems Paul has been dealing with. Therefore, he now exalts the Gospel by calling it the "glorious gospel [literally, the gospel of God's glory] of the blessed God." You can almost hear the joy and excitement in Paul's voice as he spoke those words.

Paul viewed this Gospel as that which had been committed to him as a sacred trust from God. God was trusting him! The phrase has in it the same Greek word which is translated over and over again in our New Testament by our word "believe." We are told to "believe on the Lord Jesus Christ" for salvation (John 3:16-18, 36; Acts 16:31 et al). We are to trust Him. Now Paul says that God is trusting him with the message of salvation to be proclaimed to all men. I wonder, dear reader, to what extent do you feel an irrevocable obligation to get the Gospel to those people in your "world"—those who are included in that number as far as your influence can reach? Perhaps our churches would be different if only we realized the spread of the Gospel is not an optional matter but something for which God is trusting us.

Questions for discussion:

1. How may we recognize those who are teaching "other doctrine" today, and what attitude should we take toward them?

2. What evidence will there be in the life when one follows correct doctrine?

3. How does the law apply today?

4. To whom has the Gospel been entrusted today?

2

A Sinner
Saved by Grace

I Timothy 1:12-20

THE CHAPTER OUTLINED:

  I. **The Grace of the One Who Gives Sound Doctrine**
     A. The depth to which grace has reached
     B. The purpose for which grace was given
     C. The praise of the Giver of grace

 II. **The Reaffirmation of Sound Doctrine**
     A. The charge to hold sound doctrine
     B. The shipwreck of sound doctrine

I. THE GRACE OF THE ONE WHO GIVES SOUND DOCTRINE (vv. 12-17).

A. The depth to which grace has reached (vv. 12-15).

Nobody buys hair restorer from a bald-headed man or follows the diet plan recommended by a three hundred pound woman. On the other hand when someone who has had a serious illness tells how he was cured by following the prescription of a particular doctor, everyone with the same illness wants to know the name of that doctor. So was the contrast between the "law teachers" of the opening part of the chapter and the apostle Paul. Paul was living proof of the Gospel which he preached. At the close of verse 11 he mentions the Gospel which had been committed to his trust, and this caused him to burst into praise for what it had done in his own life and to the God who made it all possible.

Paul was always very careful to give God all the glory for everything. I hear him say: "In my flesh dwelleth no good thing" (Rom. 7:18), and "by the grace of God I am what I am" (I Cor. 15:10). Here in verse 12 Paul gives thanks to Christ for three things that made him what he was. First, he gives credit to Christ who "enabled" him. This is the same word used in the familiar Philippians 4:13 where Paul states that he can do all things through Christ who "strengtheneth me." Paul knew nothing of the whining, complaining attitude which is sometimes evidenced in Christian people because they do not have this or that gift or ability. "I can't sing. I can't preach. I can't teach." So on it goes. This is complaining against God, and it is sin. Child of God, you were given everything you need to do and be what God wants in this world! Christ will enable you, and He didn't sell you short! Even Paul had to say when writing to the Romans, "So, as much as in me is, I am ready to preach the gospel . . . ." Everything that was in him was at God's disposal, and that's all God asks from any Christian.

Second, Paul thanked the Lord for counting him faithful. God recognized that the same faithful, intense, zealous Jew that persecuted Christians would be just as faithful, intense and zealous for Christ. Paul may not have been very big of stature, he may have had poor eyesight, and he may not have been very handsome (all of which have been deduced by some from Paul's epistles), but one thing he did have was invaluable to God. He was faithful! It is the one virtue that is essential in God's work. Every other talent, gift or ability is almost worthless without it. Paul tells us that it is the absolute requirement of a steward of God (II Cor. 4:2).

Last of all, Paul thanks Christ for the privilege of being in the ministry. The word "ministry" here is from the word meaning "to serve." It can be applied to any form of service for the Lord. However, Paul was here referring to his call to serve the Lord in the special way of preaching and teaching. It would correspond today to what has been ca'led "full-time Christian service," whatever the avenue of service may be—pastor, missionary, evangelist, teacher, and so forth. Paul was convinced he was in the place where God had put him.

Has God led you to teach a Sunday School class, teach child evangelism, serve as a church officer, or any other work for God no matter how menial it may seem? May God help you to view that responsibility as having been put upon you by the Lord and may you be completely faithful to it.

No doubt the heart of the great apostle hurt when he wrote the words of verse 13. Every Christian has things of the past that he wishes had never happened. But Paul felt his conduct was the worst of all. Just as there were three things in verse 12 for which he thanked the Lord, he now mentions three great sins that he sees as he looks back upon his life before his Damascus road experience. First, Paul says he was a "blasphemer." That sounds strange. Paul was always religious. He could say on another occasion, "I have lived in all good conscience before God" (Acts 23:1). Paul never blasphemed the God of Israel. There was only one Person against whom Paul had spoken—our Lord Jesus Christ. Paul now views his speech against Jesus Christ as blasphemy against God. This is one more verse in the New Testament that points to the deity of Christ. Paul also says he was a "persecutor" (cf. Acts, chaps. 8-9). So intense was the persecution that when he was converted the Christians were amazed that "he which persecuted us in times past now preacheth the faith which once he destroyed" (Gal. 1:23). The strongest term of all is reserved for last. In addition to being a blasphemer and persecutor Paul says that he was "injurious." This means to be a "wanton aggressor" and refers not only to doing injury but to the manner of spirit in which it was done. He did so with a proud, haughty, insolent spirit. Paul was not proud of these things, but he did not minimize the magnitude of his sin.

In the last part of verse 13 and verse 14 Paul points out, however, that none of these things were done intentionally against the God of heaven. These were all done "in good conscience," but it was a conscience that was wrong. This is in accord with what the Old Testament calls "sins of ignorance." Willful sin against God was not forgiven, but provision was made for sin through ignorance. See Numbers 15:27-31. However, Paul, like other religious leaders of his day should have recognized the Messiah. Paul had more spiritual light and responsibility than most, for he was an ardent student of the Scriptures—yet he did not respond.

The mercy and grace here described shine all the more brightly because they are set against the black background of verse 13. "Mercy" comes from the same root as the word "alms" (Matt. 6, Acts 3 et al), and just as the poor beggar can do nothing but plead, so the sinner can do nothing but plead the blood of Christ for forgiveness. It was not sufficient for Paul to say that he had received grace but rather that it was "exceeding abundant." This literally means "super-abounding." So great was this grace that Paul used a word to describe it that is found nowhere else in the New Testament. It was grace abounding on top of grace. We have heard a similar expression today. When someone wishes to express how wonderful a thing is, the word "fantastic" just doesn't seem to do it justice, and neither does the word "fabulous"; so he says: "That was fantabulous!" It's the same idea. Heaping superlative on top of superlative. It was "super-abounding" grace.

Verse 15 is one of the best-known verses in the New Testament and clearly declares the purpose of the coming of Christ into the world as well as the humility of the great apostle.

"Christ Jesus came into the world" stresses again the preexistence of the Saviour. This was an expression used by Jesus of himself (Matt. 9:13 and Luke 19:10) and was a favorite expression of the apostle John in speaking of the entrance of the Son of God into the world (see John 1:11 et al). The primary purpose for which Christ came, the one that overrides all the others put together, was "to save sinners." By Paul's own definition, this included everyone on earth, for "all have sinned" (Rom. 3:23). No one may escape, no matter how good he may appear in the eyes of men, because by God's standard of perfection, "every mouth may be stopped, and the whole world become guilty before God" (Rom. 3:19).

The last phrase of verse 15 has been seen by some as an exaggeration and example of false humility on the part of Paul. "Of whom I am chief"—can this be Paul speaking? However, this is simply the cry of a man who has seen himself before a holy God. Paul could not forget the days when against Christ he was a "blasphemer," "persecutor" and "injurious." The magnitude of his sin caused him to see himself as the worst sinner that God ever saved or would save. This is the cry of a truly repentant heart. Many years ago the author sat in the audience during a service of a "liberal" evangelist. After a message giving little offense to sin or the sinner, he invited people to come to the front to make a decision. He prayed for them after this fashion: "O God, bless all these wonderful people who come to thee tonight."

When a sinner comes to Christ, I submit that he doesn't see himself as a "wonderful" person! He stands like the apostle Paul alone before God as the "chief of sinners" and cries like the lowly publican, "God be merciful to me a sinner" (Luke 18:13). This is the evidence of a heart awakened, by the Holy Spirit, to its true condition. And this awareness is that which produces genuine repentance.

B. The purpose for which grace was given (v. 16).

Paul, who confessed to be the chief of sinners, says he now has become the first and foremost demonstration of God's long-suffering. God waited and waited while Paul was blaspheming, persecuting and being injurious. The depth of Paul's sin only demonstrated the depth of God's long-suffering. The word "longsuffering" used here comes from two Greek words meaning "ardor" or "temper" and "long." God was holding back His righteous ardor against sin for a long time in order that Saul of Tarsus might be saved.

If this term applied to Paul and his day, how much more does it apply to this past 2,000 years of world history and especially to the world today in which we live. I don't know about you, but I'm sick and tired of sin. I'm tired of it as I face it day by day in my own life (not that I am or want to be a hypocrite, but I'm tired of the temptations of the world, the flesh, and the devil). Moreover, I'm "sick to death" of the sin that I see round about me in this world that laughs at God and revels in wickedness. If I feel like this, I often wonder how a holy God must feel who sees sin a thousandfold with His omniscient eye that I never see. Surely He must be a God of grace and patience. And this is exactly what He is. Peter says that the primary reason why our Lord has not descended from the skies in His second coming is because God "is longsuffering to us-ward, not willing that any should perish, but that all should come to repentance" (II Peter 3:9).

The reason for that patient endurance is that a "pattern" might be given for believers in this age of grace. The word "pattern" here means "an outline, sketch or example." I recall that in the Christian elementary school with which I was formerly associated, every year just before Christmas the teacher of the fifth grade would have each of her pupils stand close to a wall with a bright light shining against the profile of the child's face. This would cast a distinct shadow on a paper on the wall. Another child would then trace around the shadow. This would then be transferred to a piece of black paper and cut out by the child. After mounting it on a piece of white paper the student would then have a lovely silhouette to present to Mother and Dad for Christmas. The shadow was a "pattern" for the silhouette. Paul declares that God's grace in saving him was a pattern for every believer in this age of grace. This pattern is big enough to include any man no matter what the nature of his sin or how great it might be. Recently I had the privilege of dealing with a man who honestly thought he was too great a sinner to be saved by Christ. What a joy it was to show him verses 15 and 16 of this chapter and tell him that Paul was the chief of sinners, and no man need fear that God would not receive him. Dear reader, that pattern includes you, too, if you are without Christ.

C. The praise of the Giver of grace (v. 17).

As Paul reflected on the depth of sin from which he had been lifted and the grace which had saved him, his heart burst forth with a doxology praising the God who did it all. This doxology begins with the phrase, "Now unto the King eternal." This is literally, "The King of the ages." The word "age" is the same word translated "world" in Matthew 28:20 ("Lo, I am with you alway, even unto the end of the world"—age). All history in the light of the Bible may be divided into various periods of time or ages. These, though lasting perhaps thousands of years, may come and go, but the God of heaven is unaffected by time and is the King of all ages. He alone is the "King." What a mockery that mere men have taken unto themselves the title "King of kings" as did the former Emperor of Ethiopia and others. One in heaven alone deserves that accolade, and someday it will be revealed as belonging to our Blessed Lord, Himself (Rev. 19:16).

This brings up the matter as to who is referred to in this verse. Is Paul referring to God the Father or to Christ? Expositors have been divided in their understanding of the matter, but I think we need not be disturbed as to which it may be. There are certain terms that would seem to apply only to the Father (as "invisible"), and yet there are others that seem to fit more aptly to the Son, such as, "immortal." However, I think this is another example of what Jesus meant when He said to Philip, "He that hath seen me hath seen the Father" (John 14:9). The two are bound as one and are inseparable. The problem of identity is solved when we apply this verse to the Triune God, not endeavoring to apply the terms to one particular Person of the Trinity.

The attributes given here of this King of the ages are "immortal, the only wise God." It is noteworthy that there are two Greek words used in the New Testament that are translated in the King James Version as "immortal." The one is "athanasia" and means "deathless." This is found in I Corinthians 15:53-54 and I Timothy 6:16. The latter passage speaks of God "Who only hath immortality." The other Greek word is "aphtharsia" found in Romans 2:7, II Timothy 1:10 and the verse we are now considering. This word means "not liable to decay, incorruptible," and is so translated in I Corinthians 9:25, 15:42,50,52-54 and I Peter 1:4 and 23. It is this word which is used in I Timothy 1:17 and refers to God as "incorruptible." This could be a reference to the resurrection body of Christ.

The word "wise" is not found in the best manuscripts and the true reading is probably "the only God," stressing not the omniscience of God but the fact that He is unique. Not only is there not another God like Him, but there is no other true God at all.

To this "only . . . God" are ascribed "honour and glory for ever." Who else is worthy of such praise? This honor and glory belongs alone to the King of the ages, and it belongs unto Him "unto the ages of the ages" (literal translation), as many ages into the future as your mind can imagine—and beyond. This grand doxology ends with an expression of strong affirmation as if to seal it all forever—"Amen."

II. THE REAFFIRMATION OF SOUND DOCTRINE (vv. 18-20).

A. The charge to hold sound doctrine (vv. 18-19).

As we would say, Paul "got carried away" from his purpose in writing when he spoke of the Gospel in verse 11 and spent the next six verses telling the story of God's grace in his own life (and what better way to "get carried away!"). He now returns to the subject of his original charge to Timothy concerning the false teachers who were teaching "other doctrine" (v. 3).

There is deep seriousness and yet tender warmth seen in Paul's admonition to Timothy, for he says the charge "I commit unto thee, son Timothy." The word "commit" means to "deposit," just as you would take your life's savings and entrust them to a bank for safe keeping. Paul is placing great responsibility on this young minister, and yet he does not do so with stern authoritarianism but rather as a father speaking to the son he loves.

This charge is reinforced by "the prophecies which went before on thee." This is not an easy phrase to understand and is made even more difficult by a rather poor translation in the King James Version. It literally speaks of the prophecies which "led the way to thee" (ASV). This undoubtedly refers to the same time and experiences as that of chapter 4, verse 14 where Timothy was admonished not to neglect the gift which had been given him "by prophecy" at the time of the laying on of hands in his ordination. This may refer to some special revelation of the Holy Spirit concerning Timothy's call and ministry such as was the case in the calling of Paul (Acts 13:2). Those prophecies led him to this present point in his life.

Paul often stressed that the Christian life and ministry is a battle in conflict with all the forces of hell (Eph. 6:10-17; I Tim. 6:12; II Tim. 4:7). We are not to "be carried to the skies on flowery beds of ease while others fought to win the prize and sailed through bloody seas." Perhaps there is a child of God reading these lines who needs to look back to his own "call" to serve the Son of God. It may be that call was to the ministry or some other phase of the Lord's service. Don't forget, that call has "led the way to thee"–brought you where you are now. If your heart is right with God, He will yet lead you through whatever trial you may be experiencing and vindicate His call and leadership in your life.

In this warfare the man of God must be careful that his own faith stays strong and his conscience clear before God. How tragic it is when we learn of one who seems to have preached and fought for one thing while his life has been something else. Paul is not talking here about holding doctrine (not "the" faith), but Timothy's own personal faith. The "good conscience" is the same as that referred to in verse 5. No matter how hard we preach or fight, we will never hear the "well done" unless our lives have been characterized by faith and a good conscience.

B. The shipwreck of sound doctrine (vv. 19-20).

The last words of this chapter are sad indeed and tell a story which has been repeated over and over again. How many there have been who have started out well but have gone off into doctrinal error and subsequently not only their relationship to God but their whole lives as well can be summed up in one word–shipwrecked. All of us have known people like this.

The shipwreck in the lives of Hymenaeus and Alexander started when they "put away concerning faith." This literally says that they "thrust from them the faith." It indicates they willfully turned their back on that body of doctrine which came from God. Result—shipwreck. Hymenaeus is referred to in II Timothy 2:17, and we learn that at least part of his error was in teaching that the resurrection was already past. This and other errors led to shipwrecked lives.

Paul says that he has delivered these unto Satan that they may learn not to blaspheme. What is meant by this is not clear except to say that some light is shed by Paul's direction to the church at Corinth concerning the man who was living in incest. There Paul counseled that the individual be "delivered unto Satan for the destruction of the flesh." The reference was to excommunication from the local church for discipline. The purpose here also seems remedial—"that they may learn not to blaspheme." In any case, the shipwreck of life was the bitter fruit of the tree of forsaking the faith.

Questions for discussion:

1. How do you picture yourself in the light of verse 15?

2. Can you look back to a time and way in which God called you to a specific task of service?

3. How do we "war a good warfare" today?

4. Is excommunication to be used by the local church today? Is it practical? Does it work?

3

Worship in the Church

I Timothy 2:1-15

THE CHAPTER OUTLINED:

I. PRAYER IN WORSHIP (vv. 1-7).

A. The method of prayer (v. 1).

In this chapter Paul turns from warnings and admonitions concerning those who would lead others into doctrinal error to instructions for the public worship service of the church. The two are not unrelated, but he has given directions concerning dealing with the false teachers and now gives directions concerning proper order in the church.

Well, if he is going to talk about the church he certainly will start out with either preaching, administration or organization. Right? Wrong! "I exhort, therefore, that first of all . . . prayers." How different from us. We affirm that prayer is the most important thing in a church and the highest privilege of a Christian, but we live as if it didn't amount to much at all. We teach our children to pray, "God is great. God is good, and we thank Him for our food." But by example we teach them, "God is great but He can wait. Gotta hurry or I'll be late." Somehow we seem to have it all backwards today. The busier we become the less time we spend in prayer. The same is true in the church. We call the prayer service the "Hour of Power," but it is the poorest attended service of the week. People will come to "fellowship hour," "family night," "recreation night" and every other event, but the prayer service goes begging for intercessors.

Paul uses four words to describe prayer. The first is "supplications," and refers in the Greek to an expression of need. It is just a matter of coming helplessly to our Heavenly Father to bring all our needs to Him. What a privilege! The second word, "prayers," is the general word used for prayer and is always used referring to deity. It is, therefore, a sacred word and carries with it the idea of worship and reverence. The next word is rather poorly translated by the word "intercessions" for it means not so much intervention on behalf of others but means "to fall in with a person, to draw near so as to converse familiarly." The idea of intercession is present, because it is when we "throw ourselves into the case of another" that we can really pray on his/her behalf. Perhaps we do well to take heed to these words not only in relation to all men but particularly concerning our rulers, which is the subject here. I wonder how many failures of our state and national leaders can be attributed to the fact that God's people failed to "throw themselves into their case" and really pray. I'm sure that if we felt a part of their burden, really felt a part of them, we would pray more and criticize less.

The last word is *eucharistias,* thanksgivings. We are told that this is to be a vital part of our prayers (cf. Phil. 4:6), and yet it usually is something that is tacked on to the multitude of our petitions. It is interesting that one of the sins mentioned in Romans, chapter 1 which describes the declension of men away from God is that they "neither were thankful" (Rom. 1:21). Thanksgiving to God is not natural to the old nature and needs to be cultivated in the heart of the Christian.

B. The subjects of prayer (vv. 1-2).

Paul first says that the church is to pray "for all men." This obviously does not mean that every man on earth is to be mentioned individually, nor does it mean a general, impersonal, all-inclusive kind of praying. It does, however, mean that all men come under the umbrella of intercessory prayer. No one is omitted. Without being impersonal, it is not improper to pray for men and nations that we have never seen and do not know. God knows them, and He answers prayer.

A specific order is given here to pray for governmental authority—"for kings and for all that are in authority." That covers every governmental official from the highest to the lowest. Paul taught that the God who is absolutely sovereign has placed each governmental official in his place, even the "bad" ones! Remember, Nero was probably on the throne when Paul wrote this, and if he could pray for Nero, surely you can pray for your governmental leaders no matter what your political persuasion might be! Because of the persecution they were experiencing, it would have been easy for Christians to allow hate to come into their hearts against political leaders. Paul knew the best antidote for hate was prayer—and that's true in every age.

One of the reasons for such prayer is "that we may lead a quiet and peaceable life in all godliness and honesty." This is not a selfish motive for prayer for governmental leaders, but it will be one of the results of answered prayer on their behalf. This desire was very real to the early Christians because of their suffering at the hands of the government. We who live in America have come to take our religious freedom for granted and thus scarcely ever thank God for it or pray that it may be preserved. We, too, may yet feel the sting of persecution for Christ and thus be caused to pray for our leaders in a new and vital way. The words "quiet" and "peaceable" here are interesting. The first speaks of tranquillity arising from no outward strife, and the second speaks of peace from within. The second may be ours in Christ Jesus no matter what outward circumstances may be, but God can provide both. "Honesty" here does not mean simply telling the truth. The idea is that of "becoming deportment, decency, decorum." The Christian's life should be characterized by dignity and good behavior.

C. The priorities of prayer (vv. 3-4)

In our praying so often the material and physical needs come first. (Witness the prayer requests at "prayer meeting"—Sister Jones has the gout, Brother Brown isn't feeling well, and so on.) The early Christians certainly had reason to pray for their physical safety and for their material needs. However, in praying for those in authority, verse 4 demonstrates that which is important to God, was important to Paul, and should have priority in our prayers. We should pray for wisdom for governmental leaders, that they will be kept from temptations of bribery, personal exaltation at the sacrifice of other men and nations, and other temptations which are uniquely theirs. However, we should pray first and most importantly of all for their salvation.

Notice that it is God's will for all men to be saved. Then why aren't all men saved? Can't God do anything He wills? The answer is found in the meaning of the word "will" in this passage. There are two Greek words used often in the New Testament both of which are translated in our Bibles by the word "will." The first is *thelo* and means "wish, desire." The second is *boulomai* and has the idea of "purpose" or "deliberate design." It is a stronger word than the first. The word used in verse 4 is *thelo*—God desires all men to be saved. He is "not willing that any should perish" (II Peter 3:9). This verse is not meant to teach universalism (that all men will eventually be saved). It is simply stating God's wish or desire. However, He does not force His salvation on any man. He has provided salvation for all, but the choice is ours to receive or reject His Son.

When we pray thus for leaders and their salvation, we will be praying in the will of God, and it will be "good and acceptable" before God. Such praying does not go unheard or unheeded. It is noteworthy that God is here spoken of as "our Saviour," or literally "our Saviour, God." This is no doubt a reference by Paul to the fact that the Roman emperor was called "Savior." In contrast to the "savior" of the Roman empire is the Christian's "Saviour"—God. The Roman emperor might be a savior in the sense of providing temporal security and prosperity, but only God can provide eternal salvation.

D. The avenue of prayer (vv. 5-7).

The avenue by which we pray is to pray to the one and only God through the one and only Mediator. Contrary to the philosophies of men, there is not one God for the Moslems, one for the Jews, one for the Christians, scores of others for men around the world, and "it doesn't make any difference how you worship just as long as you are sincere." The only God is the God who has revealed Himself through the Scriptures. He is not obscure and unknowable, but He is reaching out for men and can be known by "whosoever will."

There is likewise only one way to approach this God—through the Mediator that He has provided, "the man Christ Jesus." It is not, "You try to get to heaven in your way, and I'll go mine, but we're all working for the same place." Jesus said, "I am the way . . ." (John 14:6). He is the "mediator" between God and man. The word "mediator" here is a "go between, one who stands in the middle." Here is the answer to the longing of Job—"Neither is there any daysman betwixt us, that might lay his hand upon us both" (Job 9:33). This is exactly what Jesus Christ has done at Calvary. There He provided that a holy God and sinful man could meet through the sacrifice of Himself for our sin. And He is spoken of as "the man, Christ Jesus." I'm glad that the One who is my mediator is a man like I am. He knows my problems, my temptations, and my weaknesses. How wonderfully this is pointed out by the writer of the Book of Hebrews in 2:17 and 18.

This is the One who "gave" himself as a ransom for all. Jesus could say, "No man taketh it [my life] from me, but I lay it down of myself" (John 10:18). Jesus was not the victim of the plots of men or Satan. He freely gave Himself as a ransom for us. The word "ransom" here is precious. It literally means "that which was given instead of a slave." In other words, it was the price paid to liberate or purchase a slave. As someone has said, "He didn't just make a down payment. He paid it all."

That ransom was "for all." It included everybody. There is room here for the worst of men. Let's not get off into arguments and discussions about "limited atonement." We should not try to press such Bible teachings as the atonement, predestination, election, eternal security, the sovereignty of God, man's free will, and others to an extremity to which the Bible never goes.

This message of salvation through the ransom paid by Christ is "to be testified in due time," and that time is *now*. Although the redeeming work of Christ is timeless, the Bible says that "when the fullness of the time was come, God sent forth His Son" (Gal. 4:4). Therefore, the "due time" for the proclamation of that message is during this age of grace, from the first coming of Christ to His second coming. This gives special meaning to Paul's statement that "Now is the accepted time . . . now is the day of salvation" (II Cor. 6:2).

It was because Christ paid the ransom for all men and now is the time for the proclamation of that message that Paul was ordained to be three things—"a preacher . . . an apostle . . . a teacher." The word "preacher" here is literally "a herald." Just as a herald was sent forth to make known the proclamation of a king, so Paul had been called to proclaim the message of salvation. He was not only an apostle in official capacity, but it seems the emphasis here is upon the fact that he was one sent by God. The last calling that is mentioned is that of "a teacher of the Gentiles." This Gospel to which Paul was commissioned knew no racial or ethnic bounds. God had called him to preach primarily to the Gentiles (as Peter was called primarily to the Jews—Gal. 2:7). He carried out this ministry with all faith and sincerity ("verity").

II. PROPRIETY IN WORSHIP (vv. 8-15).

A. The instructions to praying men (v. 8).

Paul is continuing his instructions concerning prayer which were begun in verse 1. Here, in this verse, Paul now designates who is to do the praying and how they are to pray. He now says, "I will . . . ." Here is illustrated the contrast between the meanings of the two Greek words for "will" mentioned in connection with verse 4. In that verse it is stated that it is God's "will" (*thelo*—"wish, desire") for all men to be saved. Here it is Paul's "will" (*boulomai*—"purpose, design") for men to pray. Paul is giving instructions, not merely expressing what he would like to see take place in the church. The definite article is in the Greek text with the word "men" and thus should read, "I will that the men pray." By the use of the definite article (translated "the") and by the fact that the Greek word for "men" is one which means men in contrast to women, Paul is clearly pointing out that the leadership and responsibility for prayer in the public worship service is upon the men, not women. This does not mean that a woman cannot pray in a public worship service, for Paul gives instructions for a women's doing so in I Corinthians 11. However, the headship and leadership of the man is to be recognized. It should be kept in mind that Paul is giving instructions for the public worship service. This is to be distinguished from a service specifically called for prayer. Women should not hesitate to participate freely in such a service so long as the headship of the man is recognized.

The latter part of the verse speaks of the heart attitude in which prayer must be offered if it is to be effectual (cf. Ps. 66:18). Sin separates between man and God and hinders answered prayer (cf. Isa. 59:1-2). Therefore, prayer must be offered "lifting up holy hands." Although raising the hands in supplication to God is good and right, it is unlikely that Paul is talking about bodily posture in prayer because "holy" refers to a quality of life, not a part of the body. The heart must be clean and the life holy if prayer is to be heard. Neither must there be "wrath" and "doubting." Anger against men or resentment against God also makes prayer unacceptable. The word "doubting" here literally means "skeptical criticism." Have you ever prayed when down in your heart you really felt critical of the way God had dealt with you and were skeptical as to whether He was dealing fairly with you or answering your prayer?

B. The adornment of godly women (vv. 9-10).

Here is a passage that women (and men too!) would like to shy away from in this day in which we live. Read these verses over and over again and let them say exactly what they say to you, and then be not hearers of the Word only but doers (cf. James 1:22). Now lest I seem at first to be too hard on the ladies, let me point out that I do not mean that a woman is not to be attractive. I didn't say "seductive." I said "attractive"—and there's a big difference! I believe a Christian man or woman ought to be the most attractive person he or she can be for Jesus Christ whether it be in dress, manner of life, speech or whatever. Godliness is not dowdiness!

Having said this, let me now point out that a woman, however, must guard her God-given modesty. God in creation has made the man to be drawn to the woman physically, and the woman needs to recognize this and dress in such a manner as to guard her modesty. I realize that right here the Christian woman runs headlong into conflict with the "styles" of today. Men do not face this problem, at least to the same extent or same way as does the woman. And this is made all the worse by the fact that women are usually much more "style conscious" than are men. However, it is not a mere matter of style, but it is a definite moral and spiritual issue which is at stake. God says a woman is to be modest. Society says a woman is to be "liberated," "free" and "self-expressive." You have to decide whether you are going to obey God and be right with Him or conform to the world.

Paul is not saying in this passage, as some mistakenly interpret, that a woman is not to wear any gold, fix her hair, or wear attractive clothing. It says these things are not to be her "adornment." These are not to be the things that call one's attention to her. That which should adorn her life is her "good works."

C. The subjection of godly women (vv. 11-15).

As one reads on in this passage, the conflict with the "women's lib" philosophy of our day only gets worse! However, these instructions are not given because God has something against women, but because the Christian home is a picture of the union between Jesus Christ and His bride, the church (cf. Eph. 5:22-33). The man is the type of Christ in the home and the woman is a type of the church. "Therefore as the church is subject unto Christ, so let the wives be to their own husbands in every thing" (Eph. 5:24). This is the reason for the strict instruction in these verses.

It seems evident from I Corinthians 14:33-35 that women of the day were creating a disturbance in the public worship services by asking their husbands questions, apparently about what was being preached. Paul here points out that the woman is not to usurp a place of teaching and authority for which she has not been fitted either by creation or calling. The particular form of the Greek language here shows that Paul is talking about a woman being a "teacher" in the sense of being the authority of doctrine in the church. Remember, the public worship service is being discussed here. Paul is not talking about a woman teaching her children or teaching other women (cf. II Tim. 3:14; Titus 2:3), but of taking the place of the "teacher" in the local assembly of believers.

It seems to me that those groups who have "women preachers" have a real problem when they come to this passage. We are clearly told that the woman is not to teach or exercise authority over the man. This does not eliminate women teaching Sunday School classes where they are under the authority of the pastor or other men. However, it does forbid a woman to function as the pastor-teacher of a congregation of people and it also seems that it is not fitting for a woman to teach a class with both men and women present. Twice we are told that the woman is to be "in silence." This does not mean that she is to be considered as inferior to the man, for she shares equally with him in salvation and discipleship (here she is described as a "learner"). However, the primary meaning is that she is to be "in quietness," recognizing the headship of the man and submitting to authority in God's divine order.

The reason for these instructions is twofold (vv. 13-14). First of all, the order of creation gives headship to the man. The woman was made for second place. This does not mean superiority, but it does mean priority. In creation the woman was made for the man, not vice versa (I Cor. 11:9). Therefore, in creation itself man was given the place of priority, and God intends that it should remain so. Longfellow was right when he said,

> As unto the bow the cord is,
> So unto the man is woman;
> Though she bends him she obeys him,
> Useless each without the other! *(Hiawatha)*

The second reason that the woman is not to teach but to be in subjection to the man and learn from him is because of what happened at the fall in the Garden of Eden. The man was not "deceived"; but the woman, "being deceived," was in the transgression. It is interesting that the words translated here "deceived" are two different words in the Greek New Testament. The second one is a stronger form of the first word and means "to thoroughly and completely deceive." The fall into sin is shown to be the disastrous result when the woman first took a place of leadership that was never meant for her. Had she remained in a place of subordination to Adam, the fall might never have taken place. Therefore, she is instructed to take the place of a learner and one of subjection to the man. The Bible teaches and personal experience demonstrates that real happiness and fulfillment is found by either man or woman only as they take the place in life and in their homes for which the Lord created them.

The interpretation and understanding of the last verse of the chapter is not easy, and we do not intend to settle the matter in this brief study. There have been four primary interpretations. 1. That a Christian woman is promised safety in childbirth. The problem is that from Rachel until now many godly women have died in childbirth. To imply that these were less godly than those who have lived or that they were lacking in faith is nothing less than cruel. 2. That a woman who dies in childbirth will be saved. However, this goes contrary to the whole teaching of salvation by the blood of Christ and through the grace of God and does not fit with the last part of the verse which speaks of the woman's life after the childbirth. 3. That the woman's salvation "of life," her happiness is to be found in childbearing and child rearing, just as the man's is to be found in the place of leadership in the church. Many writers hold this view, and it is more in keeping with Scripture than the first two views. However, it does not fit with the force of the literal meaning of "in childbearing." The Greek here says "through the childbearing." It is not talking about a happiness of life, but the natural reading of the passage would lead us to believe that Paul is talking about eternal salvation. Since the first woman, Eve, has been under discussion and then all women who lived after her, it seems that Paul is saying that although the woman experienced the pain and suffering of childbirth as a result of her deception and fall, yet her eternal salvation is by this very means. "The childbearing" seems to point to a particular child. *The* child that a woman (Mary) was someday to bear would be the means of the salvation of mankind. "She shall be saved in [through or by means of] the childbearing." The meaning is not easy, but this seems the most literal interpretation and that which harmonizes with all of Scripture.

The chapter closes with the reminder that this salvation will be characterized by faith, love and holiness in the life of the discreet Christian woman.

Questions for discussion:

1. How does your church and its worship services measure up to the instructions concerning prayer—having a primary place, led by men and giving priority to praying for world, national and local leaders?

2. In what ways have Christian men failed to take the leadership in prayer and teaching in the local church today; and what can be done about it?

3. What should be the Christian woman's attitude toward her demeanor and dress today in the light of the present emphasis upon women's liberation?

4

What about Church Leaders?

I Timothy 3:1-16

THE CHAPTER OUTLINED:

I. THE PREACHER (vv. 1-7).

A. His character (vv. 1-3).

Although the lives of all of God's people should be characterized by holiness, God's Word lays down some special standards for those who are to be placed in positions of leadership in the church. To ignore these or seek to adjust or accommodate them to the society in which we live only leads to trouble and the sacrifice of the blessing of God.

There are two offices in the Early Church mentioned in the New Testament. They are "bishop" (meaning overseer) or "elder" (emphasizing spiritual and likely physical maturity) and "deacon" (one who serves). The terms "bishop" and "elder" referred to the same office and apply to the pastor. The bishop is dealt with first. Upon first reading, the requirement would be enough to make every pastor want to resign—"blameless." However, we can take courage when we realize it is not talking about sinless perfection (for then we all must quit), but simply and plainly it means that the man who would lead others spiritually must be above reproach. There is to be nothing in his life toward which men, either saved or unsaved, can point an accusing finger. It is interesting that the Greek word means "to take hold of." There is to be nothing that anyone can take hold of to accuse this man of God that would keep him from leading others spiritually.

The interpretations of the next qualification have ranged from saying that a single man can't be a pastor to saying that a bishop must be "married" only to the church (some Roman Catholic commentators' substantiation for celibacy of the priest). Volumes have been written and spoken as to the meaning of "the husband of one wife"; and since theologians of the centuries have not agreed, we will not attempt to be dogmatic and final in this study. In addition to the two views already mentioned, others have said that this simply prohibits polygamy, others that it means that if a pastor's wife dies he may not remarry, and still others that a pastor must not be a divorced man. Let the author just say at this point that to hold that a pastor must be married or that a pastor whose wife has died may not remarry are both pressing the word "one" to an extreme that I do not believe the text justifies. In addition, the idea that polygamy is referred to is most unlikely in view of the fact that it was forbidden on the part of all Christians (cf. I Cor. 7:2), was at the time Paul wrote forbidden in the Roman empire, and so far as we know no one in the church was guilty of this. The idea that celibacy is here taught is not even argued by most

Catholic theologians and hardly needs comment.

Therefore, the writer believes that the correct meaning is the one most obvious, namely, that a bishop is not to be a divorced man. I know the arguments that the term "one-woman man" (literal meaning) can refer to fidelity to one woman, and that there are undoubtedly men who have suffered the tragedy of divorce who are now more faithful and loyal to the woman to whom they are now married than some men who have never been divorced. This may all be true. However, the simple understanding of the passage is that the bishop is to have been married only once (unless his wife be dead, in which case other Scripture permits marriage).

As I said, the writer is sure this will not settle the differences of interpretation or change many opinions, but with love and indulgence toward others who may honestly and genuinely differ in interpretation, I present this as what I believe the term teaches.

The word "vigilant" (KJV) could better be translated "sober, temperate." It carries the idea of sound judgment. This can refer to everything from sound judgment in his personal discipline to sound judgment in doctrinal matters. May I illustrate here by saying that the word is sometimes translated "temperate." It seems inconsistent for a minister to condemn a man because he cannot quit smoking when the minister can't quit eating! Don't misunderstand. I don't believe a Christian should smoke for a number of reasons—health, testimony, habit, and so on. However, some of us have never known the grip which that habit can have on an individual; and yet we are controlled by lesser vices. Guess I'd better quit before I have "gone to meddlin'."

"Sober" means "sober-minded." Now this doesn't mean that a pastor must not have a sense of humor. Sometimes the problems become so great and the pressures so strong that the relief a good joke brings is welcomed. Paul would remind us that the business to which God has called the overseer is the most important and serious business in the world. Therefore, it needs men who are sober-minded and serious about it.

"Of good behavior" is really "orderly." This refers not only to the order of the sermons he preaches but to his whole manner of life. He surely will need this! His duties will be so many and responsibilities so great that if his life is not ordered he will accomplish the grand total of nothing. "Given to hospitality" should always characterize the Lord's people, and especially one who leads.

The bishop here described is called the "pastor-teacher" in Ephesians 4:11, and if he is to be the leader in teaching the Word of God he had better be "apt to teach." "Not given to wine" is not so much of a problem in this day when Bible-believing ministers shun all forms of alcohol (even though I learned recently of a preacher who secretly owned and operated a tavern!). In Paul's day when drinking wine was a common practice, this admonition was much needed—and it remains today. "No striker" doesn't refer to joining a union and going out on strike (though a minister could hardly fit that either), but is talking about striking someone when angry. The idea is that he is not to be violent. We need self-control, but more than that we need to be controlled by the Spirit of God. Although "not greedy of filthy lucre" is not found in every manuscript, the admonition is probably more needed today than in Paul's day. In this day it is very easy for the man of God to let economic pressures so preoccupy his thinking that money has a more important place in his life than it ought to have. Churches should do their best in meeting the pastor's need so that these pressures will not cause him to stumble and even possibly turn aside from God's call.

The words "patient" and "not a brawler" seem to me to fit together. The idea is that the pastor is not to be contentious and offensively aggressive. I do not refer to doctrinal matters. These must be held inviolate. The man of God needs to show a spirit of gentleness and patience. The last term in verse 3, "covetous" comes from two Greek words meaning "to love money." This refers to the same thing as "not greedy of filthy lucre." As someone has said: "Riches create an appetite that riches can never satisfy."

B. His home life (vv. 4-5).

How many jokes have been made about "the preacher's kids." The pastor's children are faced with problems other children do not face. It is true that "God has no grandchildren" and that even the pastor's sons and daughters must themselves be born again through a personal experience with Christ. However, the pastor has much to do with the kind of sons and daughters they will be. Do they see one man in the pulpit and another type of man at home? The pastor must so lead by authority and example that these children will want to know their father's Lord and Saviour. They are to be in subjection to him, not because he is "the boss," but because the Bible teaches God has placed him at the head of the home and holds him responsible for it. Paul says if the bishop has failed at home, he cannot possibly succeed in directing the church.

C. His maturity (v. 6).

"Not a novice" means "newly planted" and refers to a new convert. Timothy was not ordained to the ministry immediately after his conversion. It was not until Paul's second missionary journey that he passed again through Timothy's hometown and laid his hands upon him for service. The reason for this is that he be not "lifted up with pride." How easy it is for Satan to trap the preacher here! I am reminded of an incident told, I think, by Billy Sunday. Following one of his most eloquent and impassioned messages, an individual came to him and said: "That was the greatest sermon you ever preached." Billy answered, "You're too late. The devil told me that before you got here!" How easily pride can creep into the life of one who is given the responsibility to lead and teach men. This passage, by the way, sheds further light on how and why Satan fell from heaven. Satan was condemned for the sin of pride (cf. Isa. 14:12-15).

D. His reputation (v. 7).

Someone has said, "Your reputation is what men think you are; your character is what God knows you are." The leader must not only be right with God but right in the eyes of men—saved and unsaved. How many sad stories we have heard of spiritual leaders who have been dishonest, left town without paying their debts or led double lives. The cause of Christ has suffered immeasurable damage because of such things, and in most cases it takes a church years to overcome such tragedies in a community. It is true that all kinds of lies and misrepresentations may be started by the devil's crowd against the man of God who faithfully proclaims the Word of God, but we had better be sure that the Gospel is the offense and not us.

As we think back over the list of qualifications of the man who desires "the office of a bishop," it presents a pretty high standard. However, it is not a standard which is unreachable, nor is it unfitting for a man who would be an ambassador for the King of kings and Lord of lords and one who seeks to lead the people of God.

II. THE DEACON (vv. 8-10, 12-13).

A. His character (v. 8).

The office of deacon was created in Acts 6 when the apostles asked for seven men to be selected to provide for the daily ministration to the widows in order that the apostles would not have time taken from their ministry of the Word of God and prayer. This is the right kind of church organization! The bishop or elder is to give himself primarily to the study, preaching and teaching of the Word of God and prayer. Others are to be selected to care for mundane matters that must be done.

The deacons were those who served. This applies to a particular office in the church, but by extension can be applied to all who would serve in the work of the church. These standards apply to all who would serve in an official capacity.

The first requirement mentioned is that he be "grave." This does not mean a false piety and poker-faced, but rather that he is to be worthy of respect, stately and dignified. I quickly point out that this does not, however, mean austere or unbending. This is an important office, and those selected should be those held in respect and honored by the church. "Not double tongued" sounds like the common expression, "His tongue is loose on both ends." That's not far from the meaning. Since one responsibility of the deacon is to minister to those in need and therefore be involved in visitation among church members, it would be easy for him to carry tales from house to house and start rumors and gossip.

Like the bishop he must not be given to much wine. Wine was used as a common drink by people in Bible times. However, people did become drunk, and thus the warning here. This passage cannot be used as justification for drinking today when alcohol in our nation is the single greatest drug problem of our society. To this argument, Paul would say, "It is good neither to eat flesh [meat] nor to drink wine, nor any thing whereby thy brother stumbleth, or is offended, or is made weak" (Rom. 14:21). Unbelievers expect Christians to be abstainers.

The deacon is subject to the same temptation concerning money as is the pastor. Perhaps even more so because he will be in the business world from day to day. His needs will be met by his business acumen in contrast to the pastor whose needs are to be met by the people of God to whom he ministers (cf. Gal. 6:6). The deacon also must be above reproach in money matters.

B. His doctrine (v. 9).

"The mystery of the faith" spoken of here is the gospel of salvation and all the doctrine it involves. A "mystery" in the New Testament is not something "mysterious" in our sense of the word. A Bible "mystery" is something that was not previously revealed by God but has now been revealed in His own due time. The Gospel is spoken of as such a mystery (cf. Eph. 6:19). The fact that the definite article (translated "the") is before the word "faith" shows that Paul is referring to the great body of Christian doctrine. It is the same faith "once delivered unto the saints" of which Jude speaks (Jude 3). The deacon is to consider that this faith has been committed to him as a sacred trust; and it is to be held "in a pure conscience."

C. His test (v. 10).

Like the bishop, this one was not to be put into office immediately following conversion. How many churches have suffered by putting a new convert in a place of prominence simply because the individual may have been well known, had money, or for something other than a spiritual reason. The deacon was first to be proved. This does not mean some sort of formal examination or trial but simply that he has been a Christian for some time and that he has had long enough to demonstrate before other Christians that he meets the qualifications of verse 8.

D. His household (v. 12).

The same qualification concerning marriage is given for the deacon as for the bishop. Likewise, he must be the head of his house with obedient children and a well-ordered home life. I once knew a deacon whose son was about to decide to "go his own way" in disobedience to his parents. The father informed the son that if he did so the father would have to resign his position as deacon in his church because the Bible says that one qualification of a deacon is that he is to "rule his children and his own house well." The son saw the father meant what he said and was so touched by this dedication to the Lord and the Bible that he submitted to the father's will. Today that young man is an outstanding Christian leader with an international ministry.

E. His reward (v. 13).

Faithfulness is the one requirement for any servant of God (I Cor. 4:2). Without it, other qualities are nullified. To those who are faithful God always gives rewards—sometimes in this life—and the promise of eternal rewards. This verse tells us that those who fulfill the office of deacon faithfully "acquire" (better translation than "purchase"—it is not that God owes us anything) a "good standing." The Greek word translated as "degree" means "step" or "rung." It came to mean degrees of recognition or elevation, like going up steps. We might say that those who have served well "move a step up." This has to do with respect and standing in the church. It does not mean an ecclesiastic elevation of office but is simply talking about the admiration and respect rightly due a faithful servant of God. How tragic that the opposite is sometimes true. How many men have fallen from their high position of respect and dignity when some sin entered their lives. Such incidents cause angels to weep and do irreparable harm to the cause of Christ.

However, those who serve well will be rewarded; and they will be bold in faith when coming to the Throne of Grace in prayer as we are admonished to do in Hebrews 4:16 and 10:19,22. This boldness is not brazenness but is based on the finished work of Christ and the knowledge of a heart that is right with God and a faithful life.

III. THE WOMEN (v. 11).

The word used here is not deaconess but simply "women." The qualifications mentioned should certainly characterize the wives of both bishops and deacons. Four are given. Like the bishop, this one is to be "grave," worthy of respect and dignified. The Greek word for "not slanderers" is *diabolos,* one of the words used of the devil. Slander arises out of the pit of hell. Women seem to have acquired the reputation for gossip (perhaps men practice it as much, but women seem to get the credit). Her decorum must also be that of sobriety, not flippant and giddy. The last qualification embraces the entire scope of her life and service—"faithful in all things." She is to be faithful to her husband, faithful in her service, and faithful to God. Such a woman will be worthy of respect and of a place of leadership.

IV. THE SUMMARY (vv. 14-16).

A. The reason for the instructions (vv. 14-15).

Paul anticipated that he would soon come to Timothy at Ephesus. This gives weight to the theory that Paul was free from prison when writing this epistle and experienced two distinct Roman imprisonments. He does not write as a man awaiting and expecting death as he does in II Timothy. Although he expected to soon see Timothy, he felt it necessary to give these important instructions concerning church leadership. Thus Timothy would know how to conduct ("behave") himself and the church, which is "pillar and ground of the truth." "The truth" is undoubtedly that body of doctrine to which Paul has referred in chapter I and also the responsibility for the proclamation of the message of salvation through Him who is "the truth" (John 14:6). Paul is not saying that the church is the ground or foundation of salvation. Christ is that foundation (I Cor. 3:11). However, the repository and guardian of the truth in this age of grace is the church. Never forget that! Auxiliary organizations have their place and are important in the spread of the Gospel; but God's organism for the support and propagation of the truth is the church.

B. The basis of the instructions (v. 16).

The closing verse of this chapter may have been an early creedal confession or hymn. The rhythmical structure suggests this. "Without contradiction" gives the thought of something that cannot be denied. "Confessedly" would be a good way to say it. "Godliness" refers to piety toward God and is always used of men, not God. The word "mystery" here carries the same idea as in verse 9, something which heretofore was not revealed. The mystery of godliness, or that which makes a man godly, is salvation in Christ Jesus, the truth just referred to in the preceding verse. It is important to note that Paul is referring to Christ here because the word "God" is not found in this verse in the best manuscripts. The word "who" is used instead. "Who was manifest in the flesh, justified in the Spirit . . . ." However, there can be no doubt as to the One referred to. Christ is the truth of verse 15; He is the One in whom is centered the "mystery of godliness." Therefore, the sixfold description of the last part of the verse can refer to only one individual—our Lord Jesus Christ; and that One is deity.

Deity was made visible in the flesh in Christ. If men want to know what God is like, they can look at Jesus. Jesus said this in John 14:9. He was also "justified in the spirit." The word "justify" means to declare righteous or to vindicate. God is Spirit (John 4:24), and the fact that Jesus Christ was God manifest in the flesh was vindicated by the revelations of His divine spirit on several occasions in His earthly life—such as His baptism, transfiguration, and so forth. This deity was veiled behind His humanity as He walked among men, but unquestionably it shone through in His life and ministry. The fact that He was truly God was vindicated. We wonder why Paul stated our Lord was "seen of angels." This was obviously true. However, the reference is undoubtedly to the fact that Christ was greater than angels (Heb. 1), and that these mighty creatures were present at the very high points of the Saviour's earthly life and ministry, such as His birth, temptation, agony in the garden, resurrection and ascension.

Although angels witnessed His mighty acts and manifestations of deity, theirs was not to be the privilege of preaching the glorious message of salvation "unto the nations." This privilege was to be reserved for men who themselves are nothing but redeemed sinners. For nearly 2,000 years this has been our commission. As a result, Christ has been "believed on in the world." Although God's people have always been in the minority, God has always had His remnant; and they will compose a mighty host when we all get home to heaven.

The chapter closes by emphasizing that this One who walked the face of the earth is now in heaven. He was "received up in glory" (not "into" glory). Our Lord is in heaven, or as we say "in glory." This is true, but the meaning here is not so much where He went but the way in which He went—"in glory." Wouldn't you like to have been in heaven when He came home! For thirty years He walked a humble path like one of His own creation. He never did anything but good. He healed people, raised their dead and loved them. Yet He was despised and rejected. Finally, He bore the ultimate of their rejection and went to Calvary to die for them. But the grave could not hold Him. He was on the victory side of death now. The rejection, suffering and death were all over. Finally, He stepped on a cloud of glory and returned home. No earthly king or conquering general ever went home to such a welcome. The Bible doesn't describe it, but it must have been beyond all human imagination or description. Although we weren't there when it happened, we will someday see its results—the King of kings in all His glory! What a day! "Even so, come, Lord Jesus."

Questions on the chapter:

1. Is the election of officers in your church governed by the qualifications in this chapter? Should these be applied today?

2. Are we wrong in having other officers besides bishops and deacons? If so, or if not, why?

3. Does verse 15 indicate there was some kind of organization in the New Testament church?

4. Why are church officers necessary?

5

Apostasy Ahead!

I Timothy 4:1-16

THE CHAPTER OUTLINED:

I. WHAT TO LOOK FOR — "A DEPARTURE FROM THE FAITH" (vv. 1-5).

A. Marks of apostasy (vv. 1-3).

The chapter opens by warning us of a very unpleasant subject—apostasy. The New Testament warns and church history demonstrates that holding the truth and maintaining purity of doctrine is not easy. Satan is ever against the truth! Paul now instructs Timothy to be on guard for what is ahead.

"The Spirit speaketh expressly [or explicitly]." There is no need to be fooled about apostasy. The Holy Spirit has made it clear that apostasy lies ahead. This is no ambiguous double-talk. It is not . . . "you read it and get one thing out of it, and I read it and get something else out of it." The Spirit speaks explicitly on this matter. The expression "latter times" is to be distinguished from the "last days" or "last hour" of which we read in the New Testament. The "last days" is a rather technical term that refers to the entire period of time from the first coming of Christ to His second coming (cf. Heb. 1:1-2). The word "times" here refers to a short period of time, and since it is plural it thus refers to definite times of apostasy within this age of grace. No doubt these will increase and intensify as the age draws to a close.

The distinguishing mark of apostasy is not smaller church membership, less people attending church or less ecclesiastical power but that which is the heart of real Christianity—a departure from the faith. We live in a day when this is true as never before. On the day these words were written, the author watched a TV interview of one of the women who is fighting for recognition as a priest in the Episcopal church. This was especially significant to me since not long ago I had written notes concerning the qualifications of a bishop from chapter 3 of I Timothy. I wanted to ask the woman, "But what of the requirements of a bishop found in the Bible?" However, there was no need. I would know the answer before I asked. It is simple, and it is the attitude of much of Christendom today—what the Bible says doesn't really make any difference.

It is interesting that whenever men depart from the faith, they give heed to seducing (literally "deceiving") spirits and the doctrine of demons. This shows the real source of false doctrine. It is not in the superior intellect of some college professor nor in the advanced understanding of some religious leader. It comes from the pit of hell. We should not be surprised that along with the religious apostasy of our day there is a revival of demonism and Satan worship. The two go hand in hand. These "deceiving" spirits get their doctrines from the great "Deceiver" himself.

"Speaking lies in hypocrisy" refers not to the spirits who deceive but to the men who are deceived and depart from the faith. Here again the doctrine of these spirits and the men who are deceived by them are demonstrated to be "chips off the old block," the devil. Jesus termed Satan a liar and the father of lies (John 8:44).

Several different views have been given for the meaning of "having their conscience seared with a hot iron," and there is not time or space to go into all of these. However, two of them are worth mentioning and either can be true. First of all, the word "seared" comes from the Greek word "to cauterize." This is a medical term used by Hippocrates, and it is not surprising that Paul, who was very close to Dr. Luke, should use this term. One view of the meaning states that the conscience of each man was branded just as a slave was branded forever by his owner. These deceived and deceiving men bore the mark of Satan even as we who are redeemed shall have the name of the Redeemer on our foreheads for eternity. Perhaps this is so. They certainly are marked as belonging to the devil. The second view is that these have by some flagrant act of perversion of the truth forever cauterized their consciences until the truth no longer has any effect upon them. This also is true. To the author this seems to bear a very close resemblance to the unpardonable sin of which Jesus spoke. These have knowingly, willfully turned their backs on the truth and are now open to every false spirit and teaching of the devil. What a terrible situation!

Further marks of those who would depart from the faith is the fact that they would forbid marriage and certain foods (the word refers to food in general, not meat as we use the word). Both marriage and foods were created by God and, therefore, are to be used for the purpose God intended. Since it is only those "who believe and know the truth" who can give true thanks to God, we should be careful to do so. Returning thanks for our food at meals stands in danger of becoming trite for most of us since few of us have ever known what it is to be without food. It is so easy to take it for granted. However, we should always remind ourselves that every bite we eat has been created by God and graciously given to us.

B. Error of apostasy (vv. 4-5).

These verses tell us that nothing that God has created is to be rejected as being evil. Marriage is good (Heb. 13:4), and nothing God made for food is to be rejected. You may throw something away because you don't like it, but not because it is evil! These things used for food are "sanctified by the word of God and prayer" in the sense that they are recognized by the believer as being "set aside" (the basic meaning of "sanctify") for our good by God. This comes through proper instruction from His Word and from our receiving them from His hand through prayer. Jesus set the example in this when He returned thanks before feeding the multitude and at other occasions.

II. WHAT TO BE — "A GOOD MINISTER" (vv. 6-11).

A. How to prevent apostasy (v. 6).

All commentators agree that the phrase "put the brethren in remembrance" is a mild term. We might wonder why Paul did not tell Timothy to command these things to believers. It is still true that "you can catch more flies with honey than vinegar." To exercise authority and give orders, especially for a young preacher like Timothy, might be resented and rejected by believers at Ephesus. Therefore, Paul counseled a suggestion rather than a command.

If Timothy did this he would be a "good minister." This does not refer to a pastor such as our word "minister" today. Actually the Greek word is *diakonos,* exactly the same word used for "deacon" in chapter 3. The term here is not used in the sense of a church office, but the basic meaning of the word, that of serving or being a servant, is the point. Timothy was recognized as a bishop all right, but here Paul is saying that if he warns against apostasy and faithfully teaches sound doctrine he will be a good servant of God, the kind God wants and can use.

"The best defense is a good offense." This is true in spiritual matters as well as football. Paul was not merely a negative preacher or teacher (as we fundamental preachers are sometimes accused) but he also had a positive message to present. The best antidote to apostasy is to preach the truth. Therefore, in so doing Timothy would not only guard against apostasy but would be "nourished up" in the words of faith and good doctrine and so would his people. The verb here is a present participle and thus means "constantly nourishing up." How essential this is for God's people. Just as we need three square meals a day to keep us going physically, so the child of God needs daily spiritual food if he is to remain strong and grow spiritually. How many have become weak and have fallen prey to sects, cults and all sorts of false doctrines because they have failed to "study to show themselves approved unto God, rightly dividing the word of truth"

(II Tim. 2:15). If Timothy is faithful in his responsibility to warn of apostasy he will continue in the right path, because this is the one which he has "closely followed" (KJV: "has attained") up to now.

B. The best exercise (vv. 7-9).

There are some things on which a preacher shouldn't waste his time. The "myths" or "old wives fables" mentioned here are some of them. This bears a close resemblance to the "myths and endless geneologies" of 1:4. All of us have heard strange religious tales, some of which are supposedly based on the Bible, that have to do with everything from figuring out who the Antichrist is to removing warts by mysterious incantations. The best advice is—don't be bothered. Paul literally says to treat all these myths with "disdain" (the idea of the word translated "refuse"). He tells Timothy to guard the truth and fight against false doctrine, but to get himself involved in these endless myths is a waste of time.

Instead of getting involved in profitless discussions about religious myths and fables, there is something Timothy and every Christian can do with great profit. "Exercise thyself rather unto godliness." The Greek word for "exercise" here is *gumnazo*. I mention this because the reader can easily see that this is the word from which we get our English word "gymnasium." This is the place where we go to enjoy recreation and get the body muscles in tone. Paul says in the next verse that this is profitable. Although a Christian may overindulge in exercise until it also becomes a waste of time or is harmful, I'm afraid most of us neglect the proper care of our bodies in this respect. The author once read of a great preacher who said, "I go to my gymnasium with the same dedication that I go to my prayer closet." If our bodies belong to God (I Cor. 6:19-20), then we are responsible to keep them in good shape and make the best use of them. I have never been much in sympathy with the attitude, "I want to burn out for God." And some seem to try to see how quickly they can do it. I'd rather go as hard and efficiently as I can for as long as I can. To do this we must keep our bodies in shape as well as our spirits. Now I realize that in saying this I am "stepping on toes." Most of us (the author included, I confess) neglect to exercise our bodies as we should to keep them at maximum efficiency. This requires discipline.

As important as bodily exercise is, there is something vastly more important. This is the "exercise" unto godliness. This involves regular study of the Word of God, not just "hit and miss." Most of us know what it is to begin a program of physical exercise only to have it deteriorate into a "hit and miss affair." You know what happened. It eventually completely failed and you reverted to your "old flabby self." Even more are the number who have started out toward godliness but have ended the same way. How many times the pastor has heard, "Yes sir, pastor, I'm going to start reading my Bible every day, setting aside a time for prayer, participate in the evangelism program of the church and be here every time the doors are open to hear the Word of God preached and taught." He/she started out with great zeal, dedication and enthusiasm. Sometimes it lasted for days or even weeks! Then, little by little, it became a "hit and miss affair" until one was back in the same old rut. Godliness is attained only by dedication and discipline, just as physical fitness.

The reason exercise unto godliness is so much more profitable than physical exercise is that the results are so much more lasting. Bodily exercise is profitable "for a little" (literal translation). That is, it lasts only for a short time or is of little extent when compared to spiritual exercise unto godliness. Even if we keep our bodies in shape all our lives, that in itself is not very long. By contrast, godliness not only affects our lives but we shall reap the result of it in the rewards of eternity. Real life here and now is found in a right relationship to God and this life continues forever.

I make brief mention of the fact that some expositors say that when Paul made mention of bodily exercise he was not referring to bodily exercise as we think of it but was thinking of those ascetic religious practices of some false teachers of the day who laid great stress on discipline of the body as its chief expression. Although the author here does not agree with this view, it is worth mentioning because of the "spiritual experience" which devotees of such physical and mental disciplines of our day, such as yoga, claim to have. It is strange how many of the "new teachings, sciences, physical experiences," and so forth, we find already in existence in the day when the Word of God was written.

Paul concludes this admonition by emphasizing its trustworthiness and stressing that it should be received and considered by Timothy. The first part of verse 9, "This is a true saying" is literally "Faithful is the Word." This same expression has been used twice previously in the epistle (1:15 and 3:1). It is given to emphasize the importance of what has just been said. Jesus sometimes used the phrase, "He that hath ears to hear, let him hear." By this He meant, "This is the truth if you can receive it," or, "If you are willing to accept this kind of message, here it is." So Paul here emphasizes that, receive it or not, what he has just said is true and worth accepting.

C. It's worth it all (vv. 10-11).

Every bit of suffering Paul experienced and all the agony he went through for the sake of the Gospel was worth it because his trust was in the eternal God who "is the Saviour of all men, specially of those that believe"—and that God is worth trusting and never will let us down. This verse has troubled some because of the phrase, "Saviour of all men." Does this teach universalism, that all men will eventually be saved? Obviously not, because how then could He be the special Saviour of those that believe? The answer is found in understanding that by "Saviour" Paul meant even more than we attach to the meaning of the word. As Paul told the Athenians, "in him [Christ] we live, and move, and have our being." Even the very life and breath of unsaved men who may blaspheme God is a gift from God. He is even now "saving" them from a sinner's hell and giving them physical life and opportunity to be saved. In the Cult of the Caesars, which was flourishing in Paul's time, the Emperor at Rome was called "the savior of the world" by reason of the fact that he was the preserver of mankind by his beneficient reign. How much more is our God the "Saviour of all men" in the sense that *everything* good comes from His hand, even life itself. However, He is the "special" Saviour of believers in Christ. We have all the good things that a God of grace gives to unsaved men plus the priceless gift of eternal life through Jesus Christ, our Lord. The importance of what has just been said is emphasized by Paul when he admonishes Timothy to "be constantly commanding and teaching these things."

III. WHAT TO DO — "BE AN EXAMPLE" (vv. 12-16)

A. Don't leave yourself open for criticism (v. 12).

Many of us can take great comfort from the fact that Timothy may have been nearly forty years old when Paul said, "Let no man despise thy youth." You're not as old as you thought you were (or maybe, felt you were)! As Kenneth S. Wuest points out, many of the elders at Ephesus may have been older than Timothy. Forty is considered old for an athlete, young for a U.S. Senator, and very young for a Prime Minister. Timothy's actions were to be such that no one might try to push him aside because of contempt ("despise") for his life. His exemplary life in the six areas here mentioned was to command the respect which would account him worthy of spiritual leadership.

B. Be diligent (vv. 13-15).

These three verses contain four admonitions—"give attendance," "neglect not," "meditate upon," and "give thyself." The fact that Paul expected to be set free from prison is seen in the fact that he anticipated coming to Ephesus soon. Meanwhile Timothy was first of all to give attention to three things—reading, exhortation and doctrine. These all undoubtedly refer to the public worship service. Scripture was read aloud in such services and has its proper place in our services today. A. T. Robertson points out that Paul was not necessarily giving a particular order here because doctrine (teaching) usually comes before exhortation All three things mentioned are very important in a good church. The Word of God must have its central place. I sometimes think that we read about it and talk about it instead of just reading it. From this comes doctrine. We need to know what it teaches. Elsewhere Paul tells Timothy to rightly divide "the word of truth" (II Tim. 2:15). All exhortation has to be based on correct doctrine. However, we must not neglect the latter. James tells us to be "doers of the word, and not hearers only" (James 1:22). I'm afraid Bible-teaching churches are filled with people whose doctrine may be correct but whose lives are empty and powerless. Believers need constantly to be "exhorted" to obey and practice the truth they hear.

To warn those who would teach false doctrine, to teach the truth, and to give advice and counsel to the church was a great responsibility for the young man, Timothy. However, he was not asked to do this in his own strength. God had given him the necessary "gift" for his work. So it is with every child of God called to do a work for the Lord. "When God calls, He enables and equips." This gift of Timothy was apparently given at his ordination and had been revealed by prophecy to Paul or other spiritual leaders. Timothy was to use it, not neglect it.

Timothy is to carefully attend to ("meditate upon") these things and be constantly involved in them (that is, the reading, exhortation and doctrine and use of his spiritual gift). As Robertson says, he is to be "up to his ears in work and sticking to his task." If Timothy abides by these commands, his spiritual profit will be evident, and he will be the example of which Paul spoke in verse 12.

C. Watch yourself (v. 16).

No better advice could be given to a preacher, or any Christian for that matter, than that given by Paul concerning two areas—yourself and your doctrine. What you believe is tremendously important. Your eternity and your outlook on life now depend on it. However, if your conduct does not correspond to your creed, your profession will be the just ridicule of others. How every believer needs to carefully take heed to himself and his doctrine!

Paul concludes by saying that if Timothy will do as he has been advised, he will "save" himself and others. This does not take away from the fact that eternal salvation is all of God and purely by His grace. This is simply looking at salvation from the human side. Correct doctrine evidenced by a life that corresponds with it results in salvation. When Timothy taught and lived that doctrine, not only would he have salvation but many, perhaps multitudes, would also be saved because of the truth he preached and the life he lived. God may not have placed you, dear reader, in a position where multitudes will be saved as a result of your testimony and life, but God has promised to use you if you faithfully proclaim the message of salvation as found in the Word of God and back up that message by a life that demonstrates its truth.

Questions for discussion:

1. How may we recognize groups or individuals who depart from the faith?

2. What should the attitude of a Christian be toward care of his body and how should this be balanced by care of his spiritual life?

3. In what ways can you be "an example of the believer"—regardless of what your age may be?

4. Do believers have gifts today? How may a believer know what his gift is?

6

Concern for Other Christians

I Timothy 5:1-16

THE CHAPTER OUTLINED:

  I. **Respect for Others**

 II. **Responsibility for Others**
   A. Care of widows
   B. Godly vs. ungodly widows
   C. Qualifications of widows to be supported
   D. Problems of providing for young widows
   E. The high calling of young women

I. RESPECT FOR OTHERS (vv. 1-2).

This chapter opens by showing that the same attitude of love, respect and honor should characterize God's family as is true in the normal Christian home. All family members are mentioned—father, mother, brothers and sisters. The word "elder" here is not speaking of the church office but rather of an older man in the congregation and it fits with other members of the church family referred to here. Timothy is first warned against "rebuking" an older man. It is not that an older man who has sinned is not to be admonished. The word "rebuke" means to "strike with blows." It is speaking of beating with words, not with fists. Although the saying goes: "Sticks and stones may break my bones, but words can never harm me," I'm afraid much more damage has been done in this old world by words than by sticks and stones. James speaks of the damage done by the tongue. An older man who has sinned is to be admonished and discipline taken when necessary, but respect is to be shown for his age by the younger Timothy. One of the ten commandments says: "Honour thy father and thy mother," and the entire Bible illustrates that respect is to be shown to one's elders.

The same respect is to be shown to other members of the Christian family when it becomes necessary to speak to them about something that is not right. One further bit of advice is given when dealing with younger women. Timothy is to be sure that every relationship to them is "in all purity." The flesh is ever the same. The minister needs to be sure not only that his life is free from immorality but that all his actions toward women are discreet—above question and without reproach. The path of Christendom is littered with the wrecks of the lives of God's servants who have been smitten down by the devil through this means. As someone has said, "The devil will first try to spoil the Christian. If he can't spoil him, he'll try to soil him." Many have been led astray ("spoiled") by false doctrine, as illustrated in I Timothy. If the devil can't succeed in this area, he may then try to "soil" the servant of God.

II. RESPONSIBILITY FOR OTHERS (vv. 3-16).

A. Care of widows (vv. 3-4, 8, 16).

The heart of these verses is that God's people are to help supply the material needs of other Christians if there are no other believing members of the family to do so. It was the neglect of widows that caused the appointment of the first deacons. What is said here concerning care for widows can be applied to any Christians in real need. Older widows who are alone are especially to be cared for because of their destitution and old age. "Indeed" means "verily or truly" and speaks of those who are absolutely bereft of other help.

The church, however, is not a welfare agency. The church is to take responsibility to care for those who are destitute only when there are no other Christian family members to do so. It is sad that sometimes even Christians who have been loved and cared for by their parents, practically turn their backs on those parents in their hour of need. Such people need to hear these words of Paul to Timothy as well as those of James, "Pure religion and undefiled before God and the Father is this, To visit the fatherless and widows in their affliction, and to keep himself unspotted from the world" (James 1:27).

The word "nephews" of verse 4 does not mean the "nephew" as we use the word today but rather is referring to grandchildren or other relatives. When the King James Bible was translated the word "nephew" was used for grandchildren, and *Webster's Dictionary* today shows the obsolete meaning of the word to be "a lineal descendant."

"Godliness begins at home"—or at least it ought to! No matter what his profession might be or how he is "looked up to" by other members of the church or leaders in his denomination, if a man does not care for his own family "he hath denied the faith, and is worse than an infidel" (v. 8). This does not mean that he has renounced his faith in Christ, but that he has turned his back on the very responsibility that faith in Christ teaches him he should have. In fact, an unbeliever that knows nothing of the gospel of Christ or God's love knows enough to care for his family. God has put the innate knowledge in man and even animals that they are to love and care for their own. To fail to show this love and care is to deny by our actions what we profess with our lips.

In verse 16 the literal reading says, "If any woman [not man or woman as in KJV] that believeth have widows . . . ." This probably refers to a Christian woman with an unsaved husband or a younger Christian widow who has financial means to support an elderly widowed relative. An unsaved man would not recognize Christian responsibility, but a Christian woman should do so (although she is to be in subjection to her husband) if it is in her power and ability.

That the church is to care only for elderly Christian widows who have no other means of support is indicated by the fact that three times these individuals are spoken of as "widows indeed" (vv. 3, 5, and 16). First responsibility is placed upon Christian relatives and they are strongly advised to care for their widowed relatives. However, when there are no relatives to provide for the need of destitute widows, the church is to see that they are properly cared for. This is one of the social implications of the Gospel about which so much is being said in this day in which we live.

B. Godly vs. ungodly widows (vv. 5-7).

The kind of widow deserving support is seen in verse 5. She is "desolate" (literally, "alone"). Her only hope is in God. Here the word "trust" is not from the basic word meaning "faith," but rather from the word meaning "hope." Her destitution has not driven her away from God but has only served to drive her closer to the Lord, demonstrating that her faith truly is in Him and Him alone. She gives herself in prayer night and day. This is a real example of "praying without ceasing" of which Paul speaks in I Thessalonians 5:17.

Quite in contrast to this is the "merry widow"—the widow of the world. She is living a sinful, luxurious, voluptuous life. She's really "living it up." Oh yes? No. She is "dead while she liveth." This widowed woman has chosen to have her "fling," and as a sign read which was seen by the author, "The best flings in life are not free." This "fling" produced death. The Greek construction here is interesting. It says, "having died, with the present result that she is dead." She may go on with 20-20 vision and having just passed a doctor's physical examination as being in perfect health, but when she chose to live in sinful pleasure, disregarding whatever faith she may once have possessed, she died and is spiritually dead although she doesn't even know it! She thinks she's "really living," but she's dead.

Paul tells Timothy that he is to keep these facts before the Christian church that they may be kept aware of their responsibility to widows and thus not be the object of criticism ("blameless"). Younger widows (and sometimes old ones too, for there is "no fool like an old fool") need to be reminded when the difficulties of widowhood come they are not to buckle under the trials of the problems with which they are faced and thus return to the world for some sort of fleshly fling. They should not forget that such a life produces only a living death.

C. Qualifications of widows to be supported (vv. 9-10).

For reasons given in verses 11-13, younger women are not to be "enrolled." In the Early Church a widow had to reach the age of sixty before she could be supported by the church. It is assumed that before that age she could support herself, at least partially. The phrase "taken into the number" is actually a translation of one Greek word meaning "enrolled." This does not refer to church membership (younger worthy widows would hardly be denied this) but to definite lists which were kept of older, needy widows who were supported by the church. Not only must she have attained age sixty, but her life must be characterized by "good works." This would describe her whole manner of life, but four are specifically mentioned with one additional emphasis upon her entire daily walk as a Christian. First, she is to have "brought up children " The author does not believe this eliminated any widows who were childless but that it speaks of her fidelity as a mother. She was also to have "lodged strangers," a term showing her to have had a life of hospitality. She also was to have been faithful to participate in the ordinances of the church as shown by having "washed the saints' feet." The author recognizes that many see in this only a description of a life of humility, hospitality and service. However, hospitality has already been mentioned and if it is only humility and service, should not the same be showed to unbelievers? Why limit the washing to the saints if it is only humility and service. The author believes that this refers to the ordinance established by the Lord described in John 13 and is here singled out by Paul as a demonstration of the widow's devotion to the Lord and His commands.

She also is to have "relieved the afflicted," showing her mercy and sensitivity to the needs of others. The last qualification again shows her whole life and character—"diligently followed every good work." It summarizes her life as did the same description at the beginning of the verse.

D. Problems of providing for young widows (vv. 11-13, 15).

A warning now follows concerning enrolling young widows for support. They are to be refused because it is normal for them to desire to marry again. They may at first declare that they want to remain single and give themselves wholly to a life of devotion to and service for the Lord, but they may eventually be drawn toward desire for a husband and home again. The term "wax wanton" comes from the word meaning "sexual desire." Paul does not here say that this is wrong in itself. In I Corinthians and other passages of Scripture the Bible says that the marriage relationship is of God and, therefore, good. However, the problem here is that if the church enrolls a young widow for support, she may be drawn away from her "first faith" and thus the church would be supporting one who is not right with the Lord. The "first faith" here referred to may mean either a vow that she made to remain in widowhood and complete service to the Lord, thus deserving church support, or it more likely means marriage to an unbeliever which would cause her to be drawn away from the Lord and out of the will of God.

The flesh is still the same today as it was in Paul's day. Such people have "damnation" before God. This does not mean consignment to hell. Here is another illustration of the change in meanings of words since the King James Bible was translated. At that time, "damnation" simply meant to be judged or at most "condemned." The person here described stands guilty of sin against God and the church. Because of this potential problem young widows were not to be enrolled by the church for support.

Not only would the support of a young widow open the door to the problem just mentioned, but even if she does not marry, her full support would leave her free for idleness and all the problems that could come with it. "The idle brain is the devil's workshop" was true then as it is now. If the young widow was to give herself to the Lord's work, this probably would involve some house-to-house calling, and Paul warns that her visits might be for more than just evangelism! In dealing with people about Christ and their problems she would be likely to hear stories that were spoken in confidence but that were "just too good to keep." She would then become involved in gossip that could severly damage people and create great problems if she were being supported by the church. Furthermore, let it be said that this is not a sin limited to young widows! Not only do women of every age fall prey to the temptation to spread rumors and gossip, but men are guilty, too. Women get the credit for it, but men practice it with equal ability. This is illustrated by a story the author once heard of three men who were fishing. They thought it would be good while they were alone to confess their sins to one another and thus relieve their consciences. One said, "For years I have hidden the fact that I have been a slave to drink. Alcohol has had me by the throat, but no one has known it." The second said, "My weakness has been women. This has been my downfall, and no one has ever found out." The third man hastily added, "I must confess that my sin has been a gossiping tongue, and I can hardly wait to get back to town!"

As James so vividly describes, how many ships of life have been wrecked by the helm of the tongue and how many fires of gossip have wrought destruction that can never be repaired. The child of God should learn to keep confidences which have been committed to him and seek to squelch rumors which can malign character and hurt Christian testimony. This is not to say that he is to conceal or condone sin. He must do everything possible to bring the sinner to complete repentance, restitution and forgiveness, but he must not succumb to the temptation to spread gossip that would tear down rather than build up another. Widows and widowers, married and unmarried, young and old—beware.

Paul and the Ephesians knew full well that Paul knew what he was talking about, because he reminds them that some have already done the very things he has been speaking of and "are turned aside after Satan." It is interesting that the term "Satan" is used and not "Devil" or some other name. The term means "adversary," and is fitting because these widows have forsaken their former allegiance to Christ and have now become Satan's adversaries. These were once right with the Lord, but they are not so now and thus are against Him, for Jesus said, "He that is not with me is against me" (Matt. 12:30). They thus have become God's adversary. Some Bible students feel that this may not necessarily refer to Satan himself (thus making the Greek word *satana* a proper noun) but that it may simply be translated "adversary." However, the word "adversary" is used in the preceding verse (v. 14), and it is a different Greek word. It is more likely that Satan, himself, as the great adversary is referred to in this verse. The widows who have turned away from Christ in their wanton, gossiping ways have turned to Satan. There is no other alternative.

E. The high calling of young women (v. 14).

This verse doesn't exactly fit with the "women's lib" philosophy of today. It very simply states that the young women (not only young widows) are to fulfill the high calling to which women were ordained by creation. God made the woman as the one through whom the race is to be perpetuated, and no higher calling, occupation or goal may be imagined. By no means does this mean that a woman is to be "a slave of her own household, a servant for her husband and children" as some would have us believe today. The women's "libbers" would have us believe that when a woman stays at home, caring for her husband, house and family that she is being denied "the development of her creative talents." The Bible reminds us that the greatest "creative talent" that any woman ever possessed is the God-given ability to create new life. In taking the place for which she has been created she will find her greatest fulfillment, great joy and greatest peace. The author recognizes that cultures change, economics change, and in this day necessity oftentimes mandates that the wife must work outside the home. However, this should always be with reluctance recognizing that her first place of opportunity and responsibility is in her home and to her family.

Paul's wish for younger women is marriage. He does not command it but expresses it as his desire or wish (*thelo*—desire, wish. See notes on 2:4). Marriage was created by God for the joy and propagation of the human race, and is God's will for most young men and women. Celibacy is not taught in the Scripture as being superior to the marriage state. One may remain celibate for the sake of a particular ministry to which God has called him or her which would be greatly limited or impossible if the individual were married, but celibacy itself is not to be desired rather than marriage in the will of God.

The natural result of marriage will be children. This also is in the will of God. It is God's will for Christians united in marriage to bear children. Sometimes God in His own omniscience wills that this will not be so, but usually His best and greatest gift to the home will be children. In this day when overpopulation is so emphasized by much of society, having children is almost looked upon with scorn. However, the Bible teaches that "children are an heritage of the Lord" (Ps. 127:3).

Another calling and great responsibility of the young wife is to "guide the house." The literal meaning here is "to rule the house." This, however, in no way sets her above her husband, nor is this in conflict with the qualifications of bishops and deacons in 3:4 and 12 in which these are said to be ones who rule "their children and their own houses well." The Bible teaches that the husband is the God-ordained head of the household. However, he will be away at his work for most of the day, and the responsibility for ruling the children and caring for matters of the household will fall upon the wife. She should be able to do it. She should be able to take this authority. A word needs to be said concerning mothers whose only authority over the children is the threat of "just wait till your daddy comes home." She is neglecting her responsibility and backing off from what may be an unpleasant task of discipline or punishment. Moreover, she is creating in the mind of the children an image of a father whose coming is to be feared rather than joyfully longed for. Please don't misunderstand—there are times when the father must be informed of problems with the children that will need his authority and discipline, but the wife is not to use him as a crutch for problems that she ought to handle. For an excellent study and guide as to the place and responsibility of the various members of the home, the author would recommend Larry Christenson's book, *The Christian Family*. Today the home probably represents the greatest area of need, not only in our nation but probably in the church of Jesus Christ as well.

Last of all these young Christian women, wives and mothers in their households, are not "to give occasion to the adversary to speak reproachfully." There is not to be allowance for even one deed or word whereby the adversary can have a base from which to launch an attack against these women. This does not mean that she will be sinless. It does mean that she is not to make allowance for sin. Don't let the devil get his foot in the door! Often the reason we fall and sin is because we have given ourselves excuse to do so. The "adversary" here may refer to our great adversary, Satan himself, who is mentioned in the following verse.

The very practical admonitions of this chapter are given by the Holy Spirit as direction to the church, not only of Timothy's day but of ours also. They concern down-to-earth-matters—treatment and respect for older people, care of those in need, and the great responsibilities of mothers in the home. In this day of Social Security, welfare, and family problems, all society as well as the church of Christ would do well to heed the advice given here.

Questions for discussion:

1. How does the advice given in the opening part of the chapter concerning older people compare with treatment of older people in society today?

2. Can you see a difference between the attitude toward older people in the church and out of it?

3. In what way should the church today assist widows or others in need in the light of governmental social programs?

4. The Equal Rights Amendment has been much discussed in recent years. What do you think a Christian's attitude should be concerning it in the light of what the Bible says concerning the place and responsibilities of a Christian woman?

7

Let's Talk about the Pastor

I Timothy 5:17-25

THE CHAPTER OUTLINED:

    I.   How Shall We Treat Him?

    II.   "Did You Hear about the Preacher?"

    III.   Celebrity Preachers and Stomach Trouble

    IV.   As You Sow — So Do You Reap

Pastors have been talked about since the beginning of the church—some good talk and some bad talk, some good pastors and some bad pastors. From the days when the Corinthians had their "I am of Paul; and I of Apollos; and I of Cephas; and I of Christ" debate to the present hour when many congregations enjoy "roast preacher" for Sunday dinner, the pastor has been one of the favorite subjects of the church. All right, you wanted to do so—let's talk about the pastor.

I. HOW SHALL WE TREAT HIM? (vv. 17-18)

Paul now turns to the men who fulfill the office of elder or bishop in the local church. It is obvious that he is using the term "elder" as referring to the office, not simply an older man as in the opening part of the chapter. The chief responsibilities of the elders were superintending the local congregations and preaching and teaching. Different names have been given to this office down through church history, but it corresponds primarily to the "pastor" of today.

Those who "rule" well are to be accounted worthy of double honor. Although the King James Version has the word "rule" here, there is no basis for dictatorial rule over the church. The word here literally means "to stand before," or "to lead." The pastor is to direct the church, but he is to do so not only by instruction and admonition but by example as well. Someone has said there are two kinds of pastors today, shepherds and cowboys. The shepherds lead the sheep and the cowboys drive them! God wants shepherds. The word translated "pastor" in Ephesians 4:11 means "shepherd" and Peter says that the elder is to "feed [literally: shepherd] the flock of God" (I Peter 5:2).

Double honor is to be given to those who shepherd well, especially to those who "labour in the word and doctrine." He first of all is to labor. I once heard a preacher say that a pastor can be the busiest man in the world or he can be the laziest man in the world. He has no clock to punch, no boss waiting at the office to see what time he arrives, when he leaves, or if he is loafing on the job. This is one of the things that causes some critics to caustically remark, "What a job. One day a week!" This can be true if the pastor is an hireling and not a shepherd. It is strangely true that the job which carries the highest calling in the world, the greatest responsibility, and heaviest work load can also be that in which the most slothful can be found if the man so desires. However, the opposite should be true.

When a man has been called of God to pastor a group of people, he should constantly carry the realization that the spiritual welfare of this unit is in his hands. It is his responsibility to watch over them, love them, feed them spiritually, rebuke them, and encourage them that they may grow in Christ. There will be weak sheep that will demand more than their fair share of his time. There will be the spiritually sick ones that must be fed special spiritual medicine from the Word that they may be restored. There will be the impetuous that would stray or run ahead of the flock. They must be corralled. He must be careful to see that the spiritual food is sufficient for both the strong and the weak sheep, the new lambs as well as the mature sheep. This is why he must "labour" (literally: "toil to the point of exhaustion"). It will require his very best efforts under the leadership of the Holy Spirit.

The honor here mentioned is to be given especially to those who "labour in the word and doctrine." This has ever been the primary work of the minister of God. The apostles wisely recognized this at the beginning of the church. The first deacons were selected because the apostles would not be turned aside from "prayer and the ministry of the word" (Acts 6:4). A man can't expect to serve a full-course spiritual meal on Sunday morning unless he has been working in the spiritual kitchen all week!

Just recently the author heard a joke about a preacher who was asked why he never used notes when he preached. "Well," replied the preacher, "I used to study hard and have my notes all prepared. Then I'd get up to preach and the devil would cause the wind to blow, and my notes would go on the floor, and I'd get all mixed up. Now I just get up and open my mouth and neither the Lord, the devil, nor I know what I'm going to say."

The "word" here has reference to those things connected with the minister's speech, primarily preaching, and the "doctrine" is the word for "teaching." As already pointed out under the qualifications for the elder, the minister of God must be a man who is "apt to teach" (3:2).

Those who faithfully fulfill this calling deserve "double honour." Many different interpretations have been given for this phrase. Some of these are that they should be given honor as an elder and also material reward; they should be given twice as much as the widows who received assistance; they should be honored as brothers and honored as rulers; and that they should receive double pay for their work. Preachers, wouldn't it be nice if the last interpretation were the exclusive one? We could preach a lot of sermons on that theme!! The author believes that what Paul is talking about is that these elders should be given double honor—one honor because of faithfulness to the office which they hold and a second honor because they have labored so hard "in the word and doctrine." They not only should receive the honor that goes with their office, but should receive additional honor because they have labored so faithfully and diligently.

Now lest you laymen who are reading this breathe s sigh of relief that this doesn't say you have to pay the preacher, let me hasten to add I believe it does. You won't find any help for your "Lord, You-keep-him-humble-and-we'll-keep-him-poor" philosophy here. It must also be noted that the word here translated "honour" is used to speak of money in five other passages of the New Testament (Matt. 27:6,9; Acts 4:34; 7:16; and I Cor. 6:20. Look them up!) In these passages it is translated "price" or "value." Because it is so used and because of the illustration of the ox and the laborer which follows, the implication is that this one who has faithfully served the Lord and His people should be adequately cared for.

In support of his contention that elders should be properly honored, Paul quotes from the Mosaic Law in Deuteronomy 25:4 and from the words of Jesus in Luke 10:7. The second quotation is especially significant because it indicates that Luke's Gospel was already written and recognized as Scripture even though it was likely written only two or three years before Paul wrote I Timothy. This gives support to the argument that the Books of the Bible were recognized as Scripture from their very inception, not from the pronouncements of church councils or other organized bodies.

II. "DID YOU HEAR ABOUT THE PREACHER . . .?" (vv. 19-21).

The devil delights to ruin the testimony of the child of God. Someone has said that since Calvary Satan has had a twofold purpose in this world. He first of all wants to keep every sinner away from the cross of Christ by any means he may use to do it. Second, he wants to stop the testimony of every Christian any way he can. One of his many ways is to spread gossip. This will not only limit the work of the Christian because he will lose the respect of those who hear the rumor, but if the Christian hears it he may become discouraged. It is also true that the greater the opportunity for service on the part of the Christian, the greater will be the effort of the devil to falsely accuse him, both before God, as in the case of Job, and before men. Therefore, it is no surprise that Satan is a specialist at spreading lies about the preachers. This can readily be seen in the life of Paul from nearly every one of his writings. He was falsely accused of not caring for his converts, preaching for money, being filled with pride, and breaking the law. Satan saw to it that lie after lie was circulated concerning Paul, but this dedicated man of God survived them all.

The Holy Spirit here gives direction on how to deal with reports concerning sin on the part of the pastor. First of all, no such report is to be entertained unless it is verified by two or three witnesses. When two or three or more individuals are witness to sin on the part of an elder, these individuals should bring the matter personally to the church. However, these rumors which have a way of flying about from one person to another should be "nipped in the bud." They are not even to be listened to, much less repeated. It is not that such stories are to be investigated and the minister exonerated, for even then damage is done to a man and his ministry which cannot be undone. We have seen this in the secular world when a man in public office is scandalized. The scandal hits the headlines of the newspapers. Perhaps weeks or months later the man is proved innocent of the charges, but the news report of his exoneration is found, as someone has said, "on page 48 between the girdle and soap ads." The stain can never be removed. It's like the little boy who drove nails into the door of his father's barn. He was punished and made to remove the nails. The repentant little boy said, "I pulled the nails out, but the holes are still there."

This is not to say that sin on the part of an elder is to be ignored or minimized. Quite to the contrary. Because theirs is a public ministry, theirs is to be a public rebuke when sufficient witnesses are given to justify a charge of sin. The command that a minimum of two or three witnesses are to be present to establish an accusation is in keeping with the Mosaic Law (Deut. 17:6) and the words of Jesus (Matt. 18:16). When these witnesses present an accusation and such accusation is well founded, the elder is to be rebuked "before all, that others also may fear." This runs contrary to the philosophy of punishment for crime today. The elder who sins is to be publicly rebuked so that other elders may be warned against sin. This public rebuke also demonstrates before others that sin is not condoned in the life of an elder just "because of who he is." However, the admonition of the opening part of the chapter should be kept in mind, and such rebuke should be carried out with respect for the man and his office. This also guards against any pride or self-exaltation on the part of the ones who must administer the rebuke.

The absolute necessity of dealing with sin on the part of elders is further emphasized by the strong charge given in verse 21. Paul "charges" Timothy to do this. Here the meaning is to "witness or testify thoroughly." Paul wants Timothy to know that what he is saying is important and is not to be ignored.

This charge is important and is being witnessed by God, the Lord Jesus Christ and the elect angels. If Timothy fails he must someday give an account before these individuals, all of whom have heard Paul's instructions. It is interesting that this is one among several passages that teaches that angels observe the activities of God's people here on earth.

Finally, Paul warns that these instructions are to be carried out without partiality. Society today has become repulsed by reports of crimes that have gone unpunished because the guilty party "knew the right people" or "had money." Sadly, such things have happened even among God's people.

III. CELEBRITY PREACHERS AND STOMACH TROUBLE
(vv. 22-23)

The "laying on of hands" is the symbol of ordination to a specific ministry for the Lord (cf. Acts 6:6; 13:3 and I Tim. 4:14). In this case it refers to the ordination to the eldership. There are some who see in this phrase a reference to the restoration of those sinning elders mentioned in the two preceding verses. However, nowhere does the laying on of hands accompany restoration to fellowship or ministry, and there is no reason to assume that the term is used in any other than its common meaning. In fact, this precaution could probably save a lot of problems by preventing sin in the lives of elders if the selection were only made more carefully. This admonition is perhaps even more timely today than in the day it was written. How easy it is to succumb to the temptation to put in the place of leadership one who has a pleasing personality, is a good speaker, or is well known. To do so is a violation of the Word of God and often results in the church of Christ suffering harm and injury.

"Everybody's doing it." This seems to be the standard of conduct for most people today, and even Christians are influenced by it. Paul reminds Timothy that he is to "buck the current" when it comes to taking a stand against sin in his own life and in his ministry. He is not to partake of the sins in which others commonly indulge, and his is to be a life of purity both in personal conduct and in doctrine. Oh, that God's people, especially young people, might hear these words today. God's standard for His people is still moral and mental purity! We live in a day when immorality is the accepted practice of the hour and when impurity is the rule, not the exception. Purity is looked upon as archaic and something to be laughed at. However, the words of Jesus in Matthew 5:27 and 28 have never been abrogated and are still the standard to be kept before the servants of God.

Verse 23 is one verse of Scripture that the teetotalers (of which the author is one) like to skip over quickly, and those groups of Christians who drink alcoholic beverages seem to have chosen for their "life verse." Actually, it simply needs to be understood in the setting in which it was written. When Paul mentioned purity in the preceding verse, he was evidently reminded that Timothy had some stomach problems. In those days medicine was in its infancy and wine was used (and properly so) for many medical purposes. However, Timothy, for the sake of his testimony, had completely abstained. Since drinking wine was a common practice of the day and because of Timothy's physical problem, Paul advised him to use a little for medicinal purposes.

By no means is this justification for drinking alcoholic beverages today. We live in a society where alcohol is the number one drug problem of our nation. Since the drinking age has been lowered to 18, articles are constantly appearing in newspapers and magazines about the great teenage drinking problem. A Christian should take his stand against this great social evil and the only way he can consistently do so is to totally abstain from using the stuff.

For a Christian to use this verse as justification for drinking is to grasp at straws to justify a habit he wants to continue. To do so is to play with fire—setting a bad example before his own children, becoming a stumbling block before other Christians and the unsaved, and running the risk that this habit-forming drug may someday control him rather than vice versa.

IV. AS YOU SOW—SO DO YOU REAP (vv. 24-25).

The Holy Spirit is here continuing primarily to speak of elders and their selection. He points out that there are some men who immediately would be eliminated as candidates for eldership because their sins are "open, going before to judgment." Their sins are known to Timothy and everybody else; they cry like heralds preceding them to the judgment bar of God. However, Timothy need not be afraid to select elders, for the sins of some men "follow after." That is, usually by thorough examination those things which would disqualify a man from eldership will come to light. By this means those men whose lives do not measure up to what an elder should be will be eliminated. The opposite is also true. The good works of some godly men act as a herald preceding them to the judgment seat of Christ. Upon examination it will be found that these, too, are worthy of the office of eldership and thus their good works will not "be hid." God will have sufficient, qualified men to meet the need for leadership in the local church.

What is true in relation to the selection of elders is true in principle of all Christians. In another passage Paul says, "Be not deceived; God is not mocked: for whatsoever a man soweth, that shall he also reap. For he that soweth to his flesh shall of the flesh reap corruption; but he that soweth to the Spirit shall of the Spirit reap life everlasting" (Gal. 6:7-8). This passage says you can't do wrong and get by! You may get by for a while here in this life when committing certain sins, while others will bear their fruit very quickly. However, none will go unrequited by God. For some it may be suffering here and now. For others it may mean loss of reward at the Judgment Seat of Christ. Some sin is known before all here and now. Others are hid from the eyes of men but will "follow after" when they appear before the Lord.

The same manifestation is true of the godly life. Many are the rewards that come now openly before the eyes of all men for the faithful child of God. However, probably the great majority of godly works are never seen by the eyes of men. There is coming a day, however, when our God will reward even those cups of cold water that have been passed out in the name of Jesus (Matt. 10:42). In that day rewards are to be on the basis of faithfulness (I Cor. 4:2), not on the basis of who attained the prominence in this life. May each of us live his life in the light of that hour.

Questions for discussion:

1. What attitude does your church take toward the office of elder and the person who now serves as pastor? What is your attitude?

2. Can you recall examples where sinning elders have been properly accused and rebuked before the church as stated in this chapter?

3. How long should a church wait before "laying hands" on a man for the eldership?

4. What principles should guide the Christian in his conduct and practices (in the light of the verse about drinking wine)?

8

Final Instructions for the Man of God

I Timothy 6:1-21

THE CHAPTER OUTLINED:

One has only to read through this chapter to sense the burden that was upon Paul's heart for Timothy and the Christians at Ephesus. He feared for their doctrinal purity because of false teachers who had crept in among them. He longed that their lives should manifest godliness to match the doctrine they professed. The yearning of his heart is felt as we read such phrases as: "But thou, O man of God" (v. 11); "I command thee in the sight of God" (v. 13); and "O Timothy, keep that which is committed to thy trust" (v. 20). With this burden of heart Paul concludes this epistle with a final warning against false teachers and false doctrine and a last challenge to his son in the faith to be the kind of godly man that Christ would have him to be.

I. A WORD TO SLAVES (vv. 1-2).

These verses which give instructions to slaves seem almost parenthetical or out of place in an epistle which deals so much with instructions for the church and the pastor. However, we should remember that at the time of writing over half of the Roman empire was composed of those who had been brought under slavery to Caesar, or about 60 million people. Although the message of the Gospel in spirit is totally opposed to slavery, the apostles never spoke openly against it. This is an illustration of the fact that Paul felt a man's position in this life was not really the important thing. It is eternity that counts. He had written, "I have learned, in whatsoever state I am, therewith to be content" (Phil. 4:11). He wrote this when he himself was a slave of kind—in prison in Rome. He viewed every situation in life as one in which God has placed an individual when the heart is right with God. Therefore, he gave these instructions to slaves—not how to get out of their circumstances but how to live for God in the midst of their circumstances. In another passage he also instructed masters to "give unto your servants that which is just and equal; knowing that ye also have a Master in heaven" (Col. 4:1).

In the first verse instructions are given to a slave with an unsaved master whereas in verse 2 the message is to a slave with a Christian master.

The term "under the yoke" seems to indicate that these masters were unduly harsh. Nevertheless these Christian slaves were to serve them faithfully, not because of who the master is but because of the position he occupies. The master may not deserve it, but the Christian slave is to recognize the authority of the master in the culture in which he lives. To rebel would bring dishonor to God and Christian testimony.

A whole different relationship comes into being when the master is a Christian. Masters were not immediately counseled to free their slaves (cf. Philemon and Onesimus) but were to treat them with respect, honesty and equality. Christian slaves were to serve their masters well because they are brothers in Christ. Thus the slave partakes of the "benefit" of a slave who serves because he is really serving Christ in the place where he finds himself.

II. BE ON GUARD (vv. 3-10).

A. Warning against false teachers (vv. 3-5).

Paul now begins the conclusion of his epistle in the same way in which he began—by warning against false teachers. These are described as those who "teach otherwise." The Greek term here used is *heterodidaskaleo*, the same heterodoxy mentioned in 1:4. As there, he here points out that this is not some variation of the doctrine he has taught in the past, but is teaching of an altogether different kind. As Lenski says: "Paul certainly does not mince words. He does not handle men who teach differently with kid gloves. The modern indifference to different doctrine is unapostolic." This needs to be emphasized over and over again in this day when the prevailing philosophy is that "it doesn't make a difference what a man believes just so long as he is sincere."

Paul calls correct doctrine "wholesome words." The word "wholesome" comes from the same word from which we get our word "hygiene." These are "healthy" words, words which will cause a man to grow spiritually. How often the Word of God is compared to food. Peter spoke of spiritual milk (I Peter 2:2-3), and Paul spoke of spiritual milk and meat. This is the only diet that will produce a strong Christian. Make sure it is a daily part of your life.

The first three words of verse 4 give the key to about two-thirds of all spiritual problems—"He is proud." The reason sins go unconfessed is mostly because of pride. The reason sinners are unsaved is mostly because of pride. The reason a man will not admit that he is wrong in his doctrine is oftentimes because it hurts his pride to admit that he has been wrong. The false teachers here described by Paul were filled with pride.

Paul punctures the balloon of pride with which these men have pictured themselves by calling them "know nothings." It literally says that they aren't even capable of doing one bit of reflective or constructive thinking. Not much of a compliment for a proud teacher of theology! The word "doting" has the idea of "being sick," and Paul is obviously using it in contrast with the "healthy words" of sound doctrine of which he has just spoken.

Space does not permit comment on all the phrases of verses 4 and 5. For the most part they are self-explanatory. However, a couple should be emphasized. These are described as "destitute of the truth," and "supposing that gain is godliness." These people once had the truth (or at least were exposed to it) but they rejected it, and now they have been defrauded of it.

B. Warning against materialism (vv. 6-10).

Having mentioned "gain" (money), Paul now turns to materialism and its relation to godliness. He first points out that godliness with contentment is great gain. Godliness with contentment produces a "gain" that money cannot buy. In fact, how many are looking for this kind of gain who already have money. The writer of the Book of Hebrews speaks of the same thing when he says, "Let your . . . [manner of life] be without covetousness, and be content with such things as ye have; for he hath said, I will never leave thee, nor forsake thee. So that we may boldly say, The Lord is my helper, and I will not fear what man shall do unto me." Only a life of godliness can produce contentment. It comes from knowing that one is right with God and everything is committed to Him as Lord. This brings contentment. I'm afraid contentment is all too rare these days. The story is told of the old Quaker farmer who put a sign in his field that read, "I will give this field to the man who is completely contented." Before long a man stopped by to claim the field. "Are you completely contented?" asked the Quaker. "Yes, sir, I am," came the reply. "Then what dost thou want with my field?" queried the Quaker. Contentment, how rare!

The life of man is only a speck of time between two vast eternities, and yet men live as if they would exist forever as they are now. The comment was made when someone asked how much money the rich miser left when he died, "He left it all."

The words translated "food and raiment" basically have the idea of nourishment and coverings, thus including the elementary necessities of life—food, clothing and shelter. Paul is not saying that there is virtue in poverty, nor is he speaking against it. He is simply saying that if our basic needs are met, we should be satisfied.

Quite in contrast are the individuals described in verse 9, those who "will be rich." The word "will" here is not the word which is used speaking of a desire rising out of one's emotions (*thelo*—see comments on 2:4), but rather of a desire that comes from one's reasoning faculties. This isn't something that is a passing desire brought on by the emotions of the moment. Everyone, who at times has felt the pressure of financial problems, has wished that he had more money. However, the child of God who is surrendered to the Lord, relies on God to supply his needs and sets his hopes on God, not on money. The individuals of verse 9 are those whose thoughts are fastened on ways in which they can become rich. Money has become the first priority of their lives.

The problem is that the desire for riches has become the all-consuming life passion of these individuals. First money allures, then it becomes the purpose of life, and finally it controls the individual. As someone has said, "Riches create an appetite that riches can never satisfy." There's the problem. A well-known multimillionaire was once asked how much money a man must have before he would be satisfied. The man wisely replied, "Just a little more." Jesus gave a warning in Matthew 6:19-21 where he admonished his people to invest for eternity. Our treasures are to be laid up in heaven, not down here. That investment is safer than bank or bond in this world, because nothing can harm or disturb it. He reminds us that the riches of this world can be corrupted or stolen. Even more important than the fact that worldly riches can be stolen or corrupted whereas the treasure of heaven is secure, is the fact that wherever our treasure is our hearts will be also. Child of God, may our hearts and lives be centered on things that will last for eternity.

The great temptation and peril of riches is continued in verse 10. How often is this verse misquoted! The Bible does not say, "Money is the root of all evil." It says that "the *love* of money is the root of all evil." What a difference. This takes in many more people, for some of the people whom I have known who seem to love and covet money the most have very little of it! You can commit this sin while still being poor. On the other hand, the author has known people who have a great deal of money and because they realize it cannot produce happiness, they have not set their love upon it but rather use it wisely for the Lord's glory. I once had occasion to express appreciation to a man who gave $10,000 to a Christian institution. I thanked him not only for the gift but for his desire to give it to the Lord. Many people who have more money than he give not one cent to the Lord.

Neither does this verse say that all the evils of the world are the result of money (even though it may sometimes seem so!). It means that every kind of evil can come from the love of money. Dishonesty, theft, and even immorality can come to the individual because of this greed. Wars can develop among nations because of this one sin. How powerful it is.

As in the preceding verse, Paul warns that the magnetism of this sin sucks its victims into heartbreak and sorrow. It is interesting that the word "covet" means to "stretch one's self out in order to touch or grasp something" (Wuest). It is like the old picture of the carrot held in front of the horse so that the dumb animal will go forward trying to reach it. He does not know that it is tied to a stick which is tied to him so it moves when he moves. So it is with those who "stretch themselves" to get riches. They are always just a little beyond the grasp. Finally the individual may so stretch himself that this becomes his god and he errs from the faith (first by action and then perhaps by profession) and at last is impaled by the riches he has sought. He is thus pierced with "many sorrows"–literally, "consuming grief." Christians, beware!

III. PURSUE, PROTECT, PRESERVE (vv. 11-19).

A. Flee, follow and fight (vv. 11-12).

What a contrast is seen in verse 11! Timothy is to be the opposite of the individual just described. Paul calls him a "man of God." This is not an official title. It speaks of the fact that Timothy belongs to the Lord. Therefore, he is to be in experience what he has been made by the grace of God. He has become a child of the King and now should live like one. Men sometimes fail to live up to their titles. Sometimes "reverends" aren't very reverent, "ladies" aren't very ladylike, "kings" aren't very kingly and "saints" aren't very saintly. Timothy is reminded that he is a "man of God" and Paul admonishes him to "Flee, follow, and fight."

Timothy is first of all warned to flee the temptation just mentioned. Yes, even the man of God who ministers the Word can succumb to becoming a money-lover. This may all start out very innocently. His needs are the same as all men. He, too, can feel the pressure of economic problems. In addition, he has given himself to the work of the Lord and is trusting God to supply his needs. However, he may be ministering to a group of carnal Christians whose attitude is that the pastor should be no better off than the poorest church member or that the minister's poverty will help keep him godly. Money to that pastor can then become a very important thing simply because, like the old Chinese torture of letting water drip on the forehead, the "drip" of financial needs can drive him to the love of money and away from the Lord. The pastor should not be paid so lavishly that he feels no kinship to those of his congregation who daily look to the Lord for the supplying of their needs. However, on the other hand, the congregation should do all in its power to see that the needs of the pastor are met in such a way that he will not be detracted from his ministry and that money will not occupy too large a place in his life and thinking.

One way to flee the love of money is to follow the things of God. Both verbs in verse 11 are in the present imperative which means this is something that we are to be continually doing. If we are to be true men of God, we are to constantly pursue ("follow") six things—"righteousness, godliness, faith, love, patience, meekness." The "righteousness" here is not that of justification before God. This is given us by God's grace. It is that our lives shall be such before God that He can continually pronounce us righteous. This we need to pursue! We also need to grow in faith as well as grace. This is what Paul meant in Romans when he said, "The just shall live by faith" (Rom. 1:17). We go on "from faith to faith." You and I as children of God ought to trust the Lord more today than we did a year ago. As we do so "patience" will develop and increase. This word means to endure under trial. As our faith grows and we can trust the Lord in the trial, so our endurance will become stronger and stronger. In fact and experience, all six terms here mentioned fit together and grow together.

We are not only to "flee" and "follow" but also to "fight." The Christian is in a battle! Paul mentions this in Ephesians 6:10-17. The implements of our warfare are given in that passage. Our fight is not with the carnal elements of this world, but our battle is waged in the realm of "the faith." The definite article is used here in the Greek, indicating that Paul is speaking not about Timothy's personal faith as in the preceding verse but of "the faith." The late L. S. Bauman used to say that Satan is not the enemy of morals, as such. You never read of Satan causing a man to commit adultery, get drunk or steal from his neighbor. Satan gets a lot of credit for things that come out of our old sinful natures. Satan is not primarily the enemy of morals. He is the enemy of the faith! It was Satan who sowed the tares among the wheat. Dr. Bauman once said, "A woman came to me one time with a pornographic book written in France. She said that Satan had written it. I replied he did not. Some lustful old Frenchman wrote it! Satan is too busy editing Jehovah's *Watchtower* or some other heretical publication!" Above all else, Satan is the enemy of the faith. His supreme purpose in this world is to keep every man and woman, boy and girl away from the Lord Jesus Christ and faith in Him as personal Lord and Saviour. His business is opposing "the faith" and all that it involves. Remember that! When Paul came to the end of his days he could humbly and honestly say, "I have fought a good fight" (II Tim. 4:7).

Some would have us believe that Timothy was working to be saved by Paul's term, "lay hold on eternal life." Not so. Timothy is called a "man of God." He was already saved. He knew it and Paul knew it. Paul is rather challenging him to make practical in his everyday living that which he possessed as a child of God. He was to live in the light of the fact that he was a child of God and had eternal life.

B. Keep and charge (vv. 13-19).

As Paul moves to the conclusion of this epistle he sums up all he has said with a solemn charge to his son in the faith. Timothy is reminded that he is being monitored in his earthly service by none other than God the Father and our Lord Jesus Christ. Timothy, who has been admonished to steadfastness and faithfulness, is reminded that at the supreme hour of testing our Lord was steadfast and faithful. He "witnessed a good confession" before Pilate in that He testified as to his true identity (a king) and his true origin (from above). This resulted in His death which secured our salvation.

Timothy is to keep ("guard, watch, protect, preserve") the command which has been given to him concerning fidelity to pure doctrine and a godly life. He is to do so "without spot and unrebukeable."

Nothing short of complete dedication to Christ and the wisdom produced by the filling of the Holy Spirit will suffice to give discernment to "earnestly contend for the faith" in this day in which we live.

As often happens to Paul, at the mention of Deity, he is caught up in a doxology praising the God of grace and glory. Commentators have argued as to whether he is referring to God the Father or to Christ in verses 15 and 16. The author is inclined to agree with those who feel that the Father is the object here.

The final charge of the book is another warning about riches. This time it is to those who already have riches. They are warned that riches can quickly vanish and that their lives are to be invested in those things that will last for eternity. Such individuals are not to consider themselves above other brethren but are to recognize that their wealth and every other good thing is a gift of God.

Paul cannot close without one more impassioned plea to Timothy to be faithful to his call, his duty, and his Lord. He warns him to stick to the main business of preaching and teaching the faith and not to be sidetracked by useless chatter and babblings.

Questions for discussion:

1. In view of the fact that Paul did not speak out about the slavery of his day, what do you think should be the Christian's attitude toward social injustices of our day?

2. In the light of the culture in which we live, can a Christian be content with only food, clothing and shelter?

3. Can you think of experiences in your life or the lives of those you have known in which the love of money has led to evil?

4. What are some of the conditions in the Christian world which today make it necessary to "fight the good fight of faith," and how should we do so?

9

Don't Be Ashamed

II Timothy 1:1-18

THE CHAPTER OUTLINED:

Introduction to II Timothy

Careful attention is always given to the dying words of loved ones. Insofar as possible, every effort is made to carry out their last requests or instructions. The words of the book we are about to study are the last ones of the great apostle Paul. We might ask, "Can Jesus really meet your need at a time like this, Paul? Is the doctrine you have taught worth anything now? Has all your suffering been worth it?" The answers to these questions will be clearly heard in this epistle.

A totally different atmosphere prevails in the writing of this epistle from that when Paul wrote I Timothy. In that book we sense the fact that Paul expected to be set free; he is looking forward to his future ministry. The imprisonment of that time was apparently not one of harsh suffering. All is different now. The author agrees with most Bible scholars that Paul was evidently set free sometime after A.D. 64. During this time he perhaps visited Ephesus and may have actually traveled as far as Spain. However, it is now approximately three years later. The Roman madman, Nero, has set fire to the city of Rome and to remove suspicion from himself, has blamed the Christians and declared Christianity to be an illegal religion. Paul has been apprehended and is in a cold, dark dungeon in Rome awaiting execution. It is against this terrible background of suffering and human hopelessness that the aged apostle writes his beloved son in the faith.

I. PERSONAL GREETING (vv. 1-5).

A. The salutation (vv. 1-2).

Although this is a very personal letter, it is to have a place in the eternal Word of God, and the Holy Spirit through Paul sees to it that Paul's official relationship to Timothy and to the churches is established. As Paul faced death, he knew that physical death meant only a change of existence; therefore, he could speak of the "promise of life."

In this book Timothy is spoken of as Paul's "dearly beloved son." In his first epistle Paul lays emphasis on the fact that Timothy is his genuine child in the faith, but here he speaks of the tender relationship of love to this son who has meant so much to him.

B. Timothy's heritage of faith (vv. 3-5).

Paul then speaks of his own spiritual heritage and of Timothy's. If someone were to ask Paul when he began to serve God, he would no doubt have replied, "I have served God from the day of my birth." It is true that before meeting the Saviour on the road to Damascus, he was doing so in ignorance of the truth. However, he could honestly say, "I have lived in all good conscience before God until this day" (Acts 23:1). There was never a time when he willfully turned away from God.

Like Paul, Timothy also had a godly heritage, at least as far as his mother and grandmother were concerned. Although they may not have preceded Timothy in their conversions to Christ, they had been God-fearing Jews who had taught Timothy the Word of God and led him in devotion to the Lord. Thus the seedbed was prepared for the gospel of Christ to take root when Paul preached it at Lystra many years earlier. What an example this gives for parents today! In II Timothy 3:15 Paul says that from his childhood Timothy had known the Scriptures, and these Scriptures were undoubtedly faithfully taught by a mother who herself loved and served God.

I'm sorry to say that Timothy's father is not mentioned. It is supposed that he was a Gentile and was either an unbeliever or was dead. Anyway, the spiritual responsibility of the home rested on his mother. How often this is sadly true. The fact that Timothy grew up to fear the Lord vindicated her faithfulness, and God overruled the fact that Timothy had no fatherly example in spiritual things. However, in experience this seems to be the exception rather than the rule. God has placed the responsibility for spiritual headship in the home on the shoulders of the father. Dads, how about those sons who look to you?

II. BE NOT ASHAMED (vv. 6-11).

A. Stir up the gift (vv. 6-7).

Paul again reminds Timothy of the gift God had given him for the ministry to which he had been called. In I Timothy 4:14 he was told not to neglect that gift. Timothy was not sufficient in himself for the work; he needed the enablement of the gift God had given. Now he needed to rekindle the gift. Perhaps because Christians were now being persecuted throughout the Roman empire, Paul felt Timothy was in danger of weakening and needed to be prodded or encouraged.

The fact that Paul may have feared for Timothy's boldness and use of his gift is further seen in verse 7 when he reminds Timothy that the spirit which has been given to us is not one of "fear" (literally: cowardice). In the face of the threats of a Nero and his army the child of God could be bold. If this was true then in the midst of such persecution, how much more so today. About the only thing that happens today when we seek to bear such witness for Christ is that someone may give us a tongue-lashing or tell us to mind our own business. Yet we often shrink back in cowardly fear lest our feelings be hurt. What a contrast between us and Paul or Timothy!

The Spirit given us is one of "power." This is the same word from which we get our word "dynamite." It is the one used by Paul in Romans 1:16 when he says, "I am not ashamed of the gospel of Christ: for it is the power of God unto salvation." The Gospel is God's power, and He has given us that same power to proclaim it. We need only to use it, but the power is in a context of love. These gifts of power and love are exercised in the ability of a sane or sound mind. God doesn't set aside a man's sanity when he becomes a Christian (even though some believers may think so!). The spread of the Gospel or the work of God is not accomplished by human intellectual genius, but God doesn't ignore this either. As someone has said, "We need sanctified common sense."

B. Share in the sufferings (vv. 8-11).

We cannot assume from the opening statement of verse 8 that Timothy has been ashamed of the testimony of Christ. In fact, we can be sure this was not true. The particular form of the Greek language here shows that Paul is warning against something which had not yet begun. If Timothy had been ashamed, another construction of language would have been used which would have ordered him to stop it. No, Timothy was not ashamed. However, because Paul anticipated increased persecution ahead, he cautioned Timothy not to let up under pressure. Later in the epistle Paul warns that persecution will be the lot of all who will live a godly life (II Tim. 3:12). He had earlier said to the Philippians that suffering as well as faith comes from the hand of God (1:29). This is a fact which is true regardless of what generation we may live in or what form the persecution may take. When a bit of persecution comes, we act as if God had forsaken us or allowed us to be treated unfairly. Peter reminds us that this is the normal, not the strange happening (I Peter 4:12-13).

In speaking of "power" in salvation, Paul is reminded of the great salvation which has been provided for us. This is a salvation which took place in a definite point of time ("saved" is in the aorist tense, pointing to a definite time). Has there been such a time in your life? It may have been when you were so young that you can't remember the experience, but there had better be evidence now that it took place. We don't just grow up saved. How many people there are who say, "Why, I've always believed in Jesus." Yet their lives give little or no evidence of spiritual enlightenment or regeneration. Not only did God save us, but when He did so He "called us with an holy calling." This refers not only to the sovereign call of a holy God to salvation but it also refers to the holy life which should result therefrom. If we have been born of God, this new birth will be evidenced by a holy life.

We are further reminded that this great salvation is a gift of God's grace, apart from anything that we did or could do. These words sound much like Ephesians 2:8 and 9. Our salvation is according to God's own purpose and grace, and this was settled "before the world began." Literally, it says, "before eternal times." *Expositor's Greek New Testament* says that it took place before "the most remote period in the past conceivable by any imagination that man knows of." Think back just as far as you can. Then think farther, and farther, and farther. God's calling us to salvation was before any of that. The Bible says we were "chosen in Him before the foundation of the world" (Eph. 1:4, II Thess. 2:13 et al). Yes, this author believes in predestination and election. I believe it because it is in the Bible, and you can't take it out. I may not understand it all, but I would remind the reader that a sovereign and omniscient God does not have to explain Himself or all His ways to finite man. You will never with your finite mind bring Divine sovereignty and human responsibility together logically, but both are in the Scriptures and both are true. Teach them and preach them instead of trying to analyze the ways of God! Invite all men to salvation, for God is not willing that any should perish (II Peter 3:9).

This salvation, although planned from ages past, was not made clear until our Lord Jesus Christ came on the scene of human history. With His coming it has now been made manifest ("visible, brought out into the open"). Men were saved in Old Testament times by faith in God and obedience to the sacrificial offerings, but Peter says that even the prophets searched to understand some of their own prophecies concerning the grace of God and salvation (I Peter 1:10-11). All has been made plain now by the "appearing" of our Lord Jesus Christ. This appearing, while referring initially to the incarnation of the Son of God, is not limited to that. It involves all that was included in the first coming of Christ and all that is yet to transpire at His second coming. All His work on behalf of the child of God is a part of His "appearing," and it is this which has brought out into full view God's great plan of salvation for sinners.

By His work of redemption Christ has abolished death. But someone may say, "How can this be? People still die. Everyone must face death someday unless the Lord comes for us before we die." The meaning here is blessed. It is not that Christians do not experience physical death. This we may do. It is rather that death "is rendered of none effect" (the literal meaning of "abolish"). Death for Christians has lost its sting. Physical death is only a brief shift of our mode of existence. One moment is to be "in the body," the next is to be "with the Lord." This is what Jesus meant when He said to the Pharisees that the one who kept His saying, should never "see death" (John 8:51). I love what expositor Wuest says on this point. He says, "The word 'see' is *theoreo,* 'to look at with interest and attention.' The dying saint has his interest and attention so fixed on the Lord Jesus and the glories of heaven, that that stark spector, death, is only on the periphery of his consciousness." Hallelujah!

Even though he is suffering in a cold, dark dungeon, Paul's exaltation at his high calling to serve God in the proclamation of this salvation can be sensed from the words of verse 11. No earthly ambassador ever had a higher calling, and none ever viewed his position with more importance. When Paul speaks of himself as a "preacher," he used the word which means an "Imperial Herald who made a public proclamation of the Emperor's message with that formality, gravity, and authority which must be heeded" (Wuest). Thus, Paul counted every bit of suffering which he had experienced as a blessed honor for his Lord.

II. I AM NOT ASHAMED (vv. 12-14).

A. "I am not ashamed . . . I know . . . I have committed" (v. 12).

Paul had earlier challenged Timothy not to be ashamed of the testimony of the Lord or of Paul himself who was now a Roman prisoner for Christ. Like any good minister, Paul did not ask Timothy to do something that he was unwilling to do himself (quite in contrast to the lawyers of Jesus' day—cf. Luke 11:46). In spite of the fact that to renounce Christ would probably have meant his freedom, Paul joyfully declared, "I am not ashamed . . . ."

We come now to one of the greatest testimonies of assurance ever to be uttered. Paul said, "I know whom I have believed." There are two primary Greek words used in the New Testament and translated by our English word "know." The first means "to know by experience." It speaks of knowledge which is experiential and may be progressive. The second word is a stronger word and speaks of knowledge which is complete, thorough and final. It is absolute and beyond a doubt. If we could hear Paul saying these words, we would undoubtedly hear him emphasize (if not shout), "I know . . . ." The word "believed" is in the perfect Greek tense which means this belief took place in the past with the result that it is firmly settled. As Wuest says, "It is like hammering a nail through a board and clinching it on the other side. It is there to stay."

Not only does Paul say that he knows the One in whom he has believed, but he reinforces this by saying that he is "persuaded [also in the perfect tense indicating that this is unshakably settled] that he is able to keep that which I have committed unto him against that day." The word "commit" here is that used of a bank deposit. When you go to your local First National you "commit" your money with the assurance that it will be there when you want it. You don't worry about it (at least not since the Federal Deposit Insurance Corporation came into existence!). Paul had deposited his soul, his life, and his eternal destiny with the Lord Jesus Christ and he knew that He would keep it safe until "that day." The "day" mentioned here is undoubtedly the coming of our Lord when the believer is to stand before the judgment seat of Christ to receive the rewards for the things done in the body.

B. Hold (v. 13).

This verse gives strong support to the verbal inspiration of the Bible— that the very words of the Bible are important and inspired by God. The term translated "hold fast the form of sound words" indicates that Timothy was not only to be true to the basic doctrines which Paul had taught him but that he was to retain the particular words so that no deviation in doctrine would occur. Today some may glibly say that "the words of the Bible are not the important thing; it is the truth of God that counts." That all sounds very plausible until one begins to think what it means. The only way I know anything about God's truth is by what the Bible says! Those who make such statements are the same ones who deny the inspiration of Scripture but want to "get together around the Person of Christ." The only Christ I know anything about is the One I read about in the Bible! Either the Bible is the Word of God and Jesus Christ is the Son of God as presented in the Bible, or we are all on the sea of speculation.

The old nature would like to be proud because we have the truth, and we would exalt ourselves over others who are in error. Therefore, Paul tells Timothy (and us) that this holding of the truth is to be in faith and love. God gave us the faith to receive the truth in the first place, and we are to love all men as Christ loved them; so we have nothing in which to glory for ourselves.

C. Keep (v. 14).

"That good thing" is the truth or doctrine which has been entrusted to Timothy. It refers to the same thing spoken of as "sound words" in the preceding verse. This has been "committed" to Timothy (same word "commit" as in v. 12). As money is deposited in a bank, so this truth has been deposited with Timothy; and just as the banker guards the money, so Timothy is to "keep" (guard, watch or defend) the truth which has been given to him. The author is reminded of the gold deposited in Fort Knox, Kentucky. The gold is guarded so tightly that no one ever sees it. This caused rumors to arise not long ago that the gold had been removed and that the government was bankrupt. Evidence had to be given that the gold was still there—all because it was guarded so tightly. The Christian is as responsible to guard the purity of the truth of the Bible as are those in charge of Fort Knox. We need to be careful how we handle, interpret, preach, and teach the Word of God.

The only one who can enable us to guard the truth is the One who gave it—the Holy Spirit. Not only did He author the Word of God, but it is as He indwells the heart and life of the child of God that the individual has the desire to preserve the very words of Scripture. This is why liberal theologians who are not born again have no difficulty criticizing or even ridiculing portions of the Scriptures. The Word of God is precious only to the child of God who is indwelt by the Spirit of God.

III. ONESIPHORUS WAS NOT ASHAMED (vv. 15-18).

A. The unfaithful (v. 15).

How it must have hurt the heart of the great apostle as he wrote of those who had deserted him. He speaks here of those in Asia and others are mentioned in 4:10. Paul was at the end of his ministry. He was suffering. He was about to be martyred. The devil surely was trying to deal a most damaging blow to Paul by these who were once with him but now had turned away. Yet this man of God was standing firm and even rejoicing in Christ. Oh, that we who suffer far less might be as he!

B. The faithful (v. 16-18).

Even though Paul was disheartened as he thought of those who had forsaken him, he was at the same time encouraged as he thought of Onesiphorus. Evidently Onesiphorus had been a friend to Paul at Ephesus and ministered to him there. Now that Paul was in prison in Rome Onesiphorus had come to Rome and in spite of great personal danger and effort had ministered again to Paul both spiritually and physically. What a comfort this must have been to Paul as he suffered alone in the dungeon. Paul's discouragement by the thought of those who had forsaken him was offset by Onesiphorus. A preacher once said, "In every church there are those who would cause a preacher to want to resign before nightfall. But thank God, He sees to it that there are others who keep him from doing it." God knows His servants need other Christians to help and bless their lives.

Questions for discussion:

1. Does experience bear out the fact that most Christians today came from Christian homes?

2. Can you look back to experiences in your life when you have been tempted to be ashamed of the Lord? Did you fall before such temptation?

3. How may we heed the admonition to "hold fast to the form of sound words" which have been entrusted to us?

4. Are there those suffering for Christ or suffering in the flesh to whom you could and should minister as Onesiphorus did to Paul?

10

Stand Up, Stand Up for Jesus

II Timothy 2:1-13

THE CHAPTER OUTLINED:

"Stand up, stand up for Jesus, ye soldiers of the cross . . . ." With what great vigor we often sing that well-known gospel song. It appears to me that it could be used as the theme song of the second chapter of II Timothy. Here Paul shifts from the defense to the offense. In the first chapter he warns Timothy against being ashamed of the Lord. Young Timothy is not to be apologetic or defensive about the gospel of Christ. In this chapter Paul challenges him to take the initiative and go on the offense for the Saviour. As in his words to the Ephesians, Paul is telling Timothy, "having done all, to stand" (Eph. 6:13). Such words as "be strong," "endure," "war," "strive," and "suffer" characterize the chapter.

This stand for Christ is pictured in a number of illustrations in the opening part of the chapter. Let's look at them.

I. A CHRISTIAN MUST STAND LIKE A . . . (vv. 1-7).

A. Son (vv. 1-2).

Every father likes to see his son grow into a strong young man. Likewise Paul wanted his son in the faith to be strong spiritually. The word "son" used here is the same as that in 1:2 and emphasizes the genuineness of this relationship.

The admonition to "be strong" is really something that Timothy cannot do of himself. No son can simply decide that he is going to be strong. He may lift weights or do exercises to develop the muscles that he has, but strength must be produced from the right kind of nourishment and growth. This is why Paul adds "in the grace which is in Christ Jesus." In other words, he is to become strong by relying on the grace of God which only our Lord Jesus Christ can impart. John says that "of his fulness have all we received, and grace for grace" (John 1:16). This means that for every grace that is found in Christ, God has provided a similar grace for us. As we increasingly submit our lives to Him, we thus "grow in grace" and become strong.

The second verse is a very important and familiar one and it should be memorized by the reader. In his early days the late Dr. Harry Ironside was preaching concerning the necessity of Christian training and the importance of Christian schools. A lady came to him after the service and rather indignantly said: "Where in the Bible did God say anything about schools?" Dr. Ironside confidently quoted to her II Timothy 2:2. The Christian is responsible not only to grow in the knowledge of the Word of God himself, but he is to pass on to others that which he has learned and these are in turn to pass it on to still others. By the way, this is the only kind of "apostolic succession" that the Bible knows anything about. It is not a succession of administration or office but a succession of communication of spiritual truth. This is not easy. It takes a Spirit-filled life of dedicated work to train new babes in Christ and develop them into mature spiritual leaders. However, this is absolutely necessary if the body of Christ is to develop and grow.

B. Soldier (vv. 3-4).

The child of God is in a battle with the devil and his forces, and the sooner this is learned the better off we will be. Christian, Satan hates you because he hates your Lord. Therefore, we should not be surprised when we are attacked by the evil forces. Paul often speaks of this warfare. See Ephesians 6:10-17 where our spiritual armament is given. Furthermore, the more we are aggressive in battle, the more conflict we will experience. I think of this particularly in the matter of the spread of the Gospel. We may receive ridicule, may be told to mind our own business, or Satan may try to stop us in scores of other ways. Battle produces conflict and sacrifice. Therefore, we are told to "endure hardness" like a good soldier.

One way to endure the hardness is to prepare for the battle. The other day I noted an advertisement seeking to enlist men for the Marine Corps. It told how a young man enlisting in the marines would probably lose so many pounds. His waistline might be trimmed by so many inches, and so on. But after the rigorous ordeal of basic training he would also be able to run farther, lift more, think better, and look better than ever in his life. He would now be able to "endure hardness." He endured the hardness of training that he might be able to endure the hardness of conflict. So it must be with the child of God. It surely is no accident that the Holy Spirit placed the instructions concerning rightly dividing the Word of Truth in the same chapter with the charge to be a good soldier. It is only as we hide the Word of God in our heads, then in our hearts, and make it the center of our lives that we can thus become good soldiers and "endure hardness."

"So long, Sarge, I'll see you next week. I've got to take care of a business deal back home." Are these the words of a soldier? They'd better not be! The army demands that every other responsibility be dropped. The author remembers hearing a story in which Napoleon told the secret of his success to one who was reviewing the troops. At the command of Napoleon, the front row of troops marched over a cliff to their death. At a second command, the second row did likewise. "This is why Napoleon cannot be defeated," the emperor boasted.

It sometimes amazes me that God can accomplish anything at all through His people because of our lack of dedication. We sing songs of consecration and we make professions of surrender, but our lives often testify that not only are we unwilling to sacrifice for the Saviour but we don't even want to be inconvenienced. We have become so "entangled" with the things of this world that our effectiveness as a soldier of Christ is limited and sometimes nullified.

Soldiers are oftentimes drafted into the armies of this world and they serve, not for the love or honor of their commander, but because they have no choice. By contrast, God's soldiers are an all-volunteer army and our service must be because of a desire to "please him who has chosen him [us] to be a soldier." The great goal of the soldier of Christ is to hear the "well done, thou good and faithful servant" (Matt. 25:21).

C. Athlete (v. 5).

Paul now turns to the athlete for an illustration of dedication and discipline. In fact, the word translated "strive for masteries" is the Greek word from which we get our word "athlete." Paul must have loved athletics, for he often used them for illustrations. The Greek Olympic Games form the background for the illustration used here. Wuest says: "The Greek athlete was required to spend ten months in preparatory training before the contest. During this time he had to engage in the prescribed exercises and live a strictly separated life in regard to the ordinary and lawful pursuits of life, and he was placed on a rigid diet. Should he break training rules, he would, in the words of the King James Version, 'be a castaway' (I Cor. 9:27), *adokimos,* 'disqualified,' barred from engaging in the athletic contest." In recent years we have seen this illustrated in such varied athletic contests as college football and basketball teams, the Kentucky Derby horse race, and even the Soap Box Derby when entrants have been disqualified because of rule violations.

In the day when we stand before the judgment seat of Christ, our rewards will be given on the basis of faithfulness to our call and how we have "played the game." God alone knows the heart, and in that day it may be revealed that much of what appeared to be outstanding Christian service really came from a selfish motive. On the other hand, the head of that saint of God whose humble service for Christ came from a heart filled with love for Christ, though that service was unnoticed and unrewarded by men, may wear the victor's crown.

D. Farmer (vv. 6-7).

How Paul's illustration of a farmer first partaking of the fruits of his labor is intended to fit with his challenge to Timothy to be strong is not exactly clear. The soldier's enduring hardness and the athlete's sacrifices well illustrate the sacrifice required to stand for Christ. But just how does this fit with the farmer partaking of the fruit? Many explanations have been given which we will not take time or space to investigate. However, to this author, the point seems to be in the word "labor." The word used here means "to toil to the point of exhaustion, to grow weary with toil." The farmer is willing to work long, hard hours because he knows that the harvest is coming, and when it comes he, by right, enjoys the firstfruits of that labor. Surely if the farmer does this for a crop of corn, wheat or other grain, the child of God ought to give his very best in his labor for the Saviour. First of all because of his love for his Lord, and also because the rewards will be eternal.

This verse is especially applicable to ministers of the Gospel. In this high calling there is no place for indolence or shirking. It demands our very best efforts. In keeping with this, many Bible expositors feel that this verse teaches that the faithful, hard-working minister should be partaker of the first fruits of this labor in the sense that his material needs should, therefore, be met completely by the church. This would be in keeping with Paul's words in I Corinthians 9:14 where it is said "that they which preach the gospel should live of the gospel." The principle is true, but this cannot be said to be the exclusive meaning of this verse.

In the last verse of this section (v. 7), Paul says in effect, "Stop and think about what has been said." Today we are in too much of a hurry to ponder the Word of God. Meditation is a lost art. We quickly grab our five minutes (more or less) of personal devotions before rushing out the door to catch the bus. Most of us could use a lot of time just to get alone and think on the Word of God. Meditate on what you read and let the Lord apply it to your heart and life. This is where the "understanding" comes in. The things of God are not learned by mere intellectual capability. The "eyes of your understanding" are enlightened by the Spirit of God (Eph. 1:18).

II. A CHRISTIAN MUST STAND LIKE . . . (vv. 8-10).

A. Christ (v. 8).

Paul now turns from the figures of speech to the concrete example of One who took His stand without the slightest hint of failure. He uses the example of Christ not only to show His faithfulness in suffering but as the supreme illustration that reward follows faithful suffering. Christ suffered more than any of us have or could suffer. He was faithful. He turned not aside. Because He was faithful unto death the reward came—resurrection! "Wherefore God also hath highly exalted him, and given him a name which is above every name" (Phil. 2:9), and He is now "crowned with glory and honour" because of "the suffering of death" (Heb. 2:9).

Christ is spoken of as the "seed of David" to emphasize that he bore that suffering as a man. The God-man, yes, but He bore all His suffering as a man and never did He draw on any divine power to alleviate His suffering that is not available to every child of God. The point: He was faithful, and you can be, too.

This message of Christ's suffering and resurrection was the very heart of the Gospel that Paul preached. He made that clear when defining the Gospel in the opening verses of I Corinthians 15.

B. Paul (vv. 9-10).

Paul now uses himself as an example for Timothy. This is somewhat hidden by the King James Version. In verse 3 Paul told Timothy to "endure hardship." In verse 9 he now literally says, "I endure hardship" (KJV—"suffer trouble"). He used the same words to describe his own life that he used to challenge Timothy. The extent to which Paul had endured hardship is seen in the words "even unto bonds." Timothy had probably not experienced that kind of suffering. Neither have we. Paul could, therefore, point to himself as one who had gone farther in suffering than we have ever gone or probably ever will go. Blessed is that man who can point to his own life as a spiritual example.

Although Paul knew the limitations and sufferings imposed by being bound with chains, the Word of God knew no such limitations. We are reminded of the godly John Bunyan who was imprisoned for preaching the Gospel. Crowds gathered outside his prison and he preached through a barred window. A wall was erected outside the prison so people could not get to the bars. He then preached out the window, his voice carrying over the wall to those gathered to hear the Gospel. Thank God, the Word of God is not bound!

Paul knew that the salvation of men was worth any sacrifice that he could make or any suffering that he could bear. He "endured all things for the elect's sake." There is that word "election" again in the Bible. Yes, God elects, but He does not tell us in advance who the elect are. It is, therefore, our job to proclaim the Gospel to all men that the elect might "obtain eternal salvation." Again may I emphasize, Paul really believed that men were going to spend eternity either in heaven or hell, and where they were to spend it depended on whether or not they heard the Gospel and received Christ. Therefore, he sacrificed himself and everything he had to tell men the story of salvation through Christ. Oh, that you and I, child of God, will catch a burden and vision like his!

III. THE RESULT OF OUR STAND (vv. 11-12).

A. Life (v. 11).

The last three verses of this section evidently were the quotation from an early Christian hymn. They flow with rhythm and the use of the phrase "It is a faithful saying" (literally: "faithful is the word") seems to indicate a well-known saying, not something written here by Paul for the first time. The word "if" is used each time in a particular Greek construction which indicates that the condition described is actually true. It is not that we shall live with Him "on the condition that" we be dead with Him. Rather it is that "since we are dead with Him" we shall live with Him, that is, He is our life. This is in keeping with Paul's teaching in Romans 6:1-11. This is our position in Christ. It is an accomplished fact. We have died with Christ, have been buried with Him and are risen with Him. If we Christians would realize this and "reckon" (or consider) it true as Paul says in Romans 6:11, we could find the key to victory in our Christian lives.

You will note that in this section the author listed the first result of standing for Christ as "life." This does not mean that eternal life comes as a reward for taking a stand for Christ. The life meant here is that abundant life which comes alone to those who are willing to die daily to themselves that Christ may be Lord and live His life through them (cf. Gal. 2:20). As far as he was concerned he was a walking dead man. He had no life of his own, no time of his own, no possessions of his own—nothing! It all belonged to his Lord. So far as he was concerned, Saul of Tarsus was dead and Jesus Christ was living His life out through the body of Paul the apostle. Positionally, we have been crucified with Christ, but this needs to be lived out in practical experience in our everyday lives. To do so brings an abundant life that comes no other way. Surely, "if we be dead with him, we shall also live with him."

B. Royalty (v. 12).

Again, the condition is assumed to be true. We might say, "Since we are suffering we shall also reign with Him." It is true that before the crown comes the cross and before the reward comes the suffering, but it is also true that the crown follows the cross and the reward follows the suffering. God will not forget! Jesus said rewards are to be given even to those who pass out a cup of water in His name (cf. Mark 9:41). If this be true, surely He will not fail to reward those who have suffered for Him. That reward is described as reigning with Him. The Bible teaches that the Christian belongs to the royalty of heaven! We are "heirs of God, joint-heirs with Christ" (Rom. 8:17). The last chapter of the Bible says that we are to "reign" with Christ (Rev. 22:5). You probably don't look much like royalty now! Most of God's people are humble, average folks. In fact, the Bible says that God has "chosen the poor of this world rich in faith" to be "heirs of the kingdom" (James 2:5). Some day the child of God will be revealed for what he has been made by the grace of God! We can either reign up there in heaven with Christ, or we can "reign" in our own little kingdom in this world, but we can't do both. I'll take mine up there, thank you!

III. SOME WILL NOT STAND (vv. 12-13).

A. Some deny (v. 12).

Again, the form of construction used assumes the condition to be true. However, the tense of the verb is future, indicating that this had not necessarily happened yet, but that it certainly would. Some would deny. We remember that even as Paul wrote this he sadly told of Demas who had turned back to the "present world" (4:10). Jesus warned against this possibility in Matthew 10:33 and said that the result would be that He would deny these before His Heavenly Father.

B. Some are unfaithful (v. 13).

The King James Version would cause us to believe that Paul is here talking about saving faith—"if we believe not." Certainly, this is not true, because the statement "yet he abideth faithful" would be pointless. Nobody is saved apart from Bible belief. What actually occurs here is a play on words—"If we are unfaithful, yet He abides faithful." The unfaithfulness of the Christian is contrasted with the faithfulness of God. What a tremendous statement this is! In spite of our weakness, in spite of our unfaithfulness, yet God is faithful to us because He is God and must be faithful to His nature. "He cannot deny himself." What blessed security and assurance this brings.

Questions for discussion:

1. In what way does our stand for Christ differ from the stand of Paul and Timothy?

2. Do you think it was more difficult to stand then than today?

3. In what ways can Christians "deny" Christ today?

4. Can you name instances in your own life when God has been faithful to you in spite of the fact that you have been unfaithful to Him?

11

God's Workman and His Word

II Timothy 2:14-26

THE CHAPTER OUTLINED:

I. **A Hard Worker**
   A. No mere philosopher
   B. A worker in the Word
   C. Gangrene of the soul

II. **An Honorable Vessel**
   A. The unshakable foundation
   B. The usable vessel

III. **A Holy Life**

IV. **A Humble Walk**
   A. What to avoid
   B. What to do

The apostle Paul was a very practical man, and there is some very practical advice for living the Christian life in the latter part of this chapter. These words should be especially noted by those who would minister the Word of God. They could be summarized by three phrases—study the Word, stay away from sin, and serve the Lord. That's good advice. Let's see what Paul means.

I. A HARD WORKER (vv. 14-18).

A. No mere philosopher (vv. 14, 16).

The author recalls many years ago hearing a young man speak who had recently graduated from a liberal theological seminary. In his sermon he stated: "I don't want to be a great preacher. I just want to be a great thinker." It is true that before a man can preach, he must certainly think. However, it seemed to me from his message that he hadn't really spent much time in thinking or studying. More recently I heard a father complain that his son was a "professional student." Rather than studying with a particular goal in mind, he just seemed to be continually going to school. This is the type of people Paul warns against in our opening verses. They are those who spend their time wrangling about trifling matters. This sounds like the individuals Paul encountered when he came to Athens, the greatest center of learning of his day. Of them it is said that they "spent their time in nothing else, but either to tell, or to hear some new things" (Acts 17:21). One has only to be acquainted with some of the courses of study in many of our institutions of higher learning to be convinced that such "vain babblings" have not diminished but rather increased. Long doctrinal theses are written on subjects that are of little or no importance. Often the conclusions reached after weeks of research, and sometimes the expenditures of thousands of dollars of taxpayers' money, were obvious before the study was begun.

How easy it is for the preacher to become a mere philosopher and to turn aside from proclaiming the Word to a mere striving about words. The spiritual benefit and profit of such philosophical meanderings is zero. Don't waste your time. Not only is it profitless but it is actually damaging to the child of God. Those who listen with attention to such "striving about words" become "subverted." It is interesting that the word "subvert" means "overthrow" or "overturn." It came from the idea of turning over the soil with a plow. It is used in the Bible to speak of the overthrow of men and cities. The Holy Spirit here is not warning us concerning slight disruption in our spiritual progress or mere hindrance to our study of the Scriptures. The individual who becomes involved in such philosophies stands in danger of having his whole spiritual life turned upside down. How many have been the sad stories of such individuals.

Before continuing on, let us mention that when Paul warns against striving about words, he is not speaking against the study of or contending for the Word of God. Verse 15 is one of the strongest verses in the New Testament emphasizing the importance of the study of the Scriptures and our fidelity to them. The warning is against spending our time in the empty philosophies of men rather than the Word of the Eternal God.

B. A worker in the Word (v. 15).

How many a parent or teacher has used this verse to admonish his child or student to greater efforts in Bible study or other classwork. Study, study, study! Although, as we shall see, this verse definitely teaches diligent Bible study, this is not taught in the word translated "study" in our King James Bible. The meaning of this word is to "give diligence, make haste, put forth effort." As Wuest has said, Paul is here saying "Do your best, make haste, give diligence, hurry on, be eager to show yourself approved unto God." Put all these admonitions together and you have the idea of what Paul is saying. In other words, we should give everything we have to be approved before God.

The remainder of the verse contains an important and solemn admonition to the minister of the Word of God and may be applied to all who undertake the study of the Bible. He first of all must be a "workman." This comes from the word meaning to "toil to the point of exhaustion." We dare not discount the work of the Spirit in the ministry of the Word. However, the Spirit of God will not substitute for our diligent study of the Scriptures. If we are to have food for the sheep who wait before us as we stand to preach on Sunday, we must have been laboring in the study of the Word of God during the week, comparing Scripture with Scripture, digging out the truths hidden in the riches of the Word of God. This requires two things—time and effort. A minister must be a "workman." There's no other way. I like the motto of D. L. Moody—"My humble best filled with the Holy Spirit." Our humble best is worthless if we have not prayed, have not yielded ourselves to the Holy Spirit, and do not recognize that without Him we are as nothing.

We are told to "rightly divide" the Word of God. As someone has said, this does not mean cut it to pieces or fracture it! The idea here is that of "cutting straight." Since Paul was a tentmaker, he probably was thinking how important it was to cut straight lines in the rough camel's-hair cloth in order that the pieces of the tent might fit perfectly together. So it is with the study of the Word. The doctrines of the Bible fit perfectly together when studied diligently, comparing Scripture with Scripture. It is not to be presented in wordy strife (in contrast to v. 14) or to be bent to fit a particular idea the speaker desires to get across. We need to see that all our preaching, all our Sunday School teaching and other presentations are expositions of what the Scriptures say. Our responsibility is to teach and preach in such a way that these truths will be made as clear as possible to the hearts and minds of our hearers.

C. Gangrene of the soul (vv. 17-18).

In verse 16 Paul has warned that these vain babblings and strivings about words will only increase to more ungodliness. The meaning of "increase" is to "beat or chop or hammer forward." Strange progress! It leads only to ungodliness. Conduct matches creed. The test of a teaching is what it produces. This false teaching leads only to ungodliness. In verse 17 another effect of such teaching is noted. Not only does false teaching beat, hammer and chop its way forward, but it has a devastating effect upon those who become involved. It will eat away at one's soul just as a canker (literally: "gangrene") eats away at the body. The dictionary describes gangrene as "local death of soft tissues due to loss of blood supply." The blood carries no food to the cells, therefore, they die. So it is with the poor soul who feeds upon the vain babblings and empty words of these theological philosophers. There is no milk or meat of the Word of God and gangrene of soul sets in. If not arrested in time it becomes fatal. The only remedy is complete eradication of the infected flesh. Nothing but a complete eradication of the false doctrine and restoration of the Word of God which is food for the soul will rescue the perishing soul. Christian, beware of the smooth talk and pleasing personalities of the cult leaders who come knocking at your door. And beware of the glib tongue of the sophisticated liberal preacher who stands behind a pulpit mouthing these "vain babblings" which are not in accord with the Scriptures. Such teachings "beat, hammer and chop" their way forward, and the effect upon your soul will be that of spiritual starvation and gangrene.

Hymenaeus was mentioned in I Timothy 1:20 as one of the individuals that Paul evidently had to put out of the church because of his false teaching. Philetus is not mentioned elsewhere. The dangerous doctrine they proclaimed was that the resurrection was already past. Perhaps they were teaching that the only resurrection is a spiritual one which occurs in connection with the new birth. This may have sounded very pleasing to their hearers. After all, they may have been teaching the new birth. Isn't that the most important message we can proclaim? This all sounds very well until we begin to see the implications of what is meant. If there is no physical resurrection of the Christian, then Christ did not rise (as Paul states in I Cor. 15:16). If Christ did not rise, He died as any other man and His death could not pay for our sins. He is not the Son of God and there is no new birth to be experienced. Like false preachers and teachers today, the teaching of Hymenaeus and Philetus may have sounded very plausible until the meaning is seen in its full light. These have completely missed the mark (KJV "erred") of the truth and the disastrous results are that some are listening to them and their faith is being overthrown. This is a catastrophe (the word "subverting" in verse 14 is the word from which we get our word "catastrophe"). How these false cults love to prey on new converts and those weak in the faith. Presenting themselves as teachers of new light or additional truth, they overturn the faith of these weak individuals rather than adding to it. Beware!

II. AN HONORABLE VESSEL (vv. 19-21).

A. The unshakeable foundation (v. 19).

Although when we first read the word "foundation" in this verse, our minds immediately go to I Corinthians 3:11 in which Christ is spoken of as our foundation, I do not think He is referred to here. It is more likely that the true church is pictured as the foundation. This is in keeping with the picture of the church given in I Timothy 3:15 where the church is called "the pillar and ground of truth" and also in keeping with the subject of which Paul has been speaking. Jesus said, "I will build my church; and the gates of hell shall not prevail against it" (Matt. 16:18). Not all the false teachers, demons in hell or the devil himself can stop this work of Christ in the world.

This foundation has a twofold seal. First of all, "the Lord knoweth them that are his." This has to do again with election. God has chosen and will preserve His own. False teachers, or not, God will keep His people. This is God's side of the seal. The second is man's side—"Let every one that nameth the name of Christ depart from iniquity." The second evidence that God's church is standing and will continue to do so is the fact that there are those true children of God who manifest by their lives that God's church is alive and well. Thank God, He always has His people. We may sometimes feel like Elijah, that we are the only ones left, but then He shows us that in our day, too, there are 7,000 that have not bowed the knee to Baal.

B. The usable vessel (vv. 20-21).

We live in the day of "throw-away" eating! Cups, plates, forks, knives, spoons, napkins and in fact almost everything we use for eating is disposable. When it is soiled it is never to be used again. This has led to the greatest litter problem in world history. By contrast, one of the few valuable things our family has is some china given to my wife by her mother on our wedding day and some crystal and silverware, much of which were wedding presents. These are anything but disposable. In fact, after dinner my wife always sees that these are washed first and separate from any other dishes, pots or pans. They are carefully wiped and stored in the china cabinet before the rest of the dishes are done. These are vessels unto honor. They are not to be endangered by washing them with the rest of the utensils used in the meal. This is the basis of Paul's illustration here.

The "great house" here is the professing church. In it are teachers and professors—both true and false. Those false teachers are pictured as contaminated vessels, not to be given any honor. They are to be avoided and the church is to be purged from them.

The only solution is separation from such individuals. If the minister will do so, he will thus be "sanctified," set apart for God. Wuest here makes an important application. He says, "Here it has direct application to the obligation of a pastor to refuse to fellowship in the work of the ministry with another pastor who is a Modernist. The perfect tense speaks of a past action on his part of separating himself from such, and his present confirmed practice of maintaining that separation." These words were first written by Mr. Wuest over twenty years ago, and they need to be heeded today more than ever.

III. A HOLY LIFE (v. 22).

These words sound much like Paul's words to Timothy in 6:11 of his first epistle. The spiritual qualities mentioned here which we are to pursue cannot be stressed too strongly. By contrast, we are told to "flee youthful lusts." Someone has well pointed out that we are told to "resist the devil"

(James 4:7), but when it comes to the lust of the flesh, the Bible tells us to "flee" (see also I Cor. 6:18). One of the best protections that God has given us against immorality are two good legs for running! This is exactly what Joseph did when tempted to sin by Potiphar's wife (Gen. 39) and what David failed to do when he fell into sin with Bathsheba (II Sam. 11). Remember—flee.

The positive side of the verse now follows. The best way to avoid sin is to be busily engaged in godly pursuits. It is still true that "an idle brain is the devil's workshop." The "righteousness" here spoken of is not our right standing before God. That comes by grace alone through faith in the finished work of Christ. This rather refers to a righteous life. John speaks of this when in Revelation 19:8 he sees the bride of Christ "arrayed in fine linen, clean and white: for the fine linen is the righteousness of saints." Although we are clothed in the righteousness of Christ by the grace of God, apparently in that day the redeemed will also be clothed in white linen symbolizing our righteous lives in Jesus Christ. This is the event when we ought to want to be among the best dressed.

The other virtues which Paul here tells Timothy to pursue (faith, love and peace) sound like a portion of the fruit of the Spirit mentioned in Galatians 5:22. We should have a hunger for these things in our lives. As we do so and submit ourselves to the Holy Spirit He will produce these things in us. In so doing we will be numbered among those who "call on the Lord out of a pure heart." This is in contrast to those whose lives are taken up with vain babblings and thus produce only ungodliness.

IV. A HUMBLE WALK (vv. 23-26).

A. What to avoid (v. 23).

We dare not minimize the danger facing the minister of the Gospel in getting sidetracked from his main business. He has been called to preach and teach the Word of God. It is very easy to get involved in discussions about things that don't really matter. They are spoken of as "foolish," or "stupid." Moreover they come from people who are "unlearned." This word is the negative form of the word meaning to "train a child." In other words, these individuals who spend their time in debating such questions have not learned the very fundamental facts as to what is really important. They waste their time in endless discussions which profit nothing and ignore the great privilege and responsibility of the study and proclamation of God's Word. The result of such questionings is not spiritual growth or the spread of the Gospel but only strife. Such things Timothy is to "disdain" (literal meaning, "avoid").

B. What to do (vv. 24-26).

The words of these verses are meant especially for the pastor or minister of God, but every Christian who would be a "servant" of Jesus Christ does well to take heed to their counsel. The word "servant" is used by Paul many times in referring to himself or another who would serve Jesus Christ. It is the word meaning "bondslave" and speaks of the servitude of slavery. Over half the Roman world of Paul's day was composed of slaves, forced to be so by their Roman masters. However, those who would serve Jesus Christ most effectively must take their places as willing bondslaves, ready to obey their Lord completely.

The closing verses of this chapter give a beautiful picture of proper contending "for the faith" (Jude 3). While standing irrevocably for the truth of God, the servant of the Lord must do so without any sense of personal pride or attitude of self-achieved superiority. There will be times when the minister of God must, like John the Baptist, denounce sin or heresy with thunderous tones, but he must always be sure that this is for the sake of the Gospel and glory of God, not for the exaltation of the flesh.

This passage says that the servant of God is not to "strive." This means "fight," or "wrangle." The author has sometimes heard a minister of the Gospel described as "a real fighter." Men who acquire such a reputation had better be sure their fight is for the Lord and led of the Spirit and not one of personal prestige or pride.

Although he may hate the error taught by those opposing the truth, the true servant of God must be gentle to friend and foe alike. He must know the truth of God, be able to teach it, and be patient in doing so; for it is only then that he will cause those involved in false teaching to see the error of their way.

This kind of firm but gentle contending for the faith may result in the rescue of those who have been led astray and perhaps even some who are teaching false doctrine. God, by grace, may grant a spiritual awakening and repentance may take place in such individuals. "May recover themselves" means literally to "awaken as out of a drunken stupor." How many individuals have said and done things (even violent crimes) which they never would have done when sober and for which they experienced bitter remorse when awaking out of their drunkenness. So is the enlightenment that comes to the individual who, by the power of the Spirit of God, sees the truth of salvation by grace through our Lord Jesus Christ. He has been delivered from the "snare" of the devil and set free in Christ.

May we be long-suffering and kind in dealing with eternal souls about their salvation, realizing that we, too, were once as blind and deluded as they. Also we should realize that the salvation of one soul is worth whatever patience and long-suffering may be required in our presentation of the truth of the Gospel.

Questions for discussion:

1. Can you recall experiences in your own life when you have endeavored to present the Word of God to an individual or group but have found it has been turned aside to "vain babblings"?

2. Evidently Paul had put Hymenaeus out of the church. Do you think such action should be taken today? What would constitute grounds for such action? What grounds did Paul use for excommunication?

3. Paul spoke of the faithful minister of God as "purging" himself from "vessels" of "dishonor." This referred to separation from false teachers! In the light of religious conditions of our day, how and when should we separate ourselves from others who claim to be Christian?

4. Can you give an example of someone who was involved in false teaching but has been "recovered" because of the faithful, gentle teaching of some Christian?

12

The Last Days

II Timothy 3:1-17

THE CHAPTER OUTLINED:

I. The Signs of Apostasy
   A. Time of apostasy
   B. Marks of apostasy

II. The Sort of Men Described
   A. Their actions
   B. Their predecessors
   C. Their destiny

III. The Saint of God in Contrast
   A. Paul's life and suffering
   B. Our lives and suffering
   C. It won't get easier

IV. The Scriptures — Sufficient for All Days
   A. Persist in the Scriptures
   B. The origin and purpose of the Scriptures

In this chapter we come to one of the great prophecies of the Bible and one of the most familiar portions of the New Testament. It has been used as a text for many great sermons on prophecy. The author has often stated that if the editor of any leading newspaper of our nation were to be asked to write a list of twenty characteristics of the day in which we live, he could do no better than to copy the first five verses of II Timothy, chapter 3.

I. THE SIGNS OF APOSTASY (vv. 1-5).

A. Time of apostasy (v. 1).

The time is described as "the last days." Many an unbeliever or skeptic when hearing sermons from this chapter replies with disdain: "I've always heard about those things. Conditions have always been like that." This is true and can be understood in the light of the meaning of the term "last days." This is a term with a special meaning in the New Testament. It refers not so much to the last twenty-four hour days before the coming of Christ, but is used to speak of the whole period of time from His first coming to His second coming. The message of God to men in this age of grace has been the message of salvation through faith in the Son of God (cf. Heb. 1:2). Therefore, the whole period of time from Calvary to the present is spoken of as "the last days." It is a proper term because these are the last days of God's dealing with this old world. As one views history in the light of the Bible, it may be divided into various periods of times of dispensations. We say that we are in the age or dispensation of grace. After this there are no more ages to come. Christ is coming to rule and reign.

B. Marks of apostasy (vv. 2-5).

The first characteristic is placed where it should be—at the head of the list because perhaps it is the basis of all the rest. "Lovers of their own selves" is said to be the basis of all other sin—selfishness. How this speaks of our day! The attitude today is, "What's in it for me?" "What do I get out of it?" There was a day when the craftsman took pride in his work. The prevailing philsophy today is, "How long do I have to work to get it done, and what do I get out of it when it's finished?" Self-lovers. This is followed by a second characteristic closely allied to it—covetousness. The Greek word comes from two other words meaning "fond of" and "silver," thus "fond of silver." Paul warned against the love of money in I Timothy 6:10. In our day we have seen materialism grip its icy fingers around the throat of our nation until it is all but strangled to death. Not only have governmental figures succumbed to bribes and sacrificed the honor and security of our nation, but the philosophy of the average man seems to be, "I'm going to cheat the other fellow before he cheats me." The moral breakdown caused by the love of money is unparalleled in the history of our nation.

"Boasters, proud, blasphemers" may well be taken together. When men deify themselves, they humanize God. As man is exalted, God is degraded. Men today are arrogant, blasphemous. In our generation the "God is dead" theology even dared to rear its ugly head. In Romans 3:18 Paul concludes his characterization of the heart of a sinner by saying, "There is no fear of God before their eyes." As these words sum up the description of the heart in rebellion against God, it should be no surprise that this becomes one of the distinguishing marks of the close of the age of grace.

"Disobedient to parents" is especially noteworthy in this day when juvenile delinquency is at an all-time high. Ingratitude is a sin which God hates. It, too, is mentioned in Romans 1, verse 2, as a mark of the sinful heart. "Thank you" is a phrase which is fast slipping from the vocabulary of our society.

"Unholy" refers to complete disregard for things sacred. One has only to watch the desecration of the Lord's Day or listen to the jokes about God and religion on TV to see the extent to which this has gone in our day.

"Without natural affection" seems especially descriptive of the time in which we live. We live in a day when people are bestowing more love on dumb animals than they do the offspring of their own bosom. Millions are being spent on dog and cat foods. The author recently viewed on TV a news report showing a convention of proprietors of pet cemeteries— complete with caskets, markers and even "funeral services" for pets! By contrast, atrocities against members of one's own family are increasing.

"Trucebreakers." These words are being written on the very day that South Vietnam has fallen to communist control. The news programs have been filled with interviews asking whether our allies now feel that the United States can longer be trusted. My purpose is not to debate the war in southeast Asia or how it was fought but only to point out that for the first time in her history the United States has broken and is breaking treaties for the sake of expediency. "False accusers" reminds us of the charges and counter charges hurled by governmental officials and the news media at national leaders and governmental agencies. However, this may refer to accusations which may be made against Christians as the coming of our Lord nears. We live in a day when the rights of every minority group in the country seem to be carefully protected except those of one group of people—Bible-believing Christians. This group seems to watch their rights and privileges slip away. Can false accusations be far behind?

"Incontinent" means "lacking in self-control"—the "playboy" philosophy, if you please. The new morality has completely taken over and according to its concepts there is no such thing as the sin of the flesh today. The word "adult" has become synonymous with complete licentiousness and profligacy. I submit that part of adulthood at maturity is self-control! The "incontinent" become wild, like untamed animals—"fierce." They are also "despisers of those that are good." Like Daniel who was hated because no fault could be found in him, God's people will be increasingly hated because they are good and men of the world are bad, not because they are bad and other men are good.

"Traitors, heady, highminded"—all speak of self-will which seeks only to exalt the individual regardless of what injury is caused to anyone else. Betray anyone, do anything, say anything because the individual is exalted above any god or man. "Highminded" comes from a term meaning "smoke" or "mist." He has his "head in the clouds" all right—a cloud of self-exaltation which has blinded him to everything and everyone else.

"Lovers of pleasure more than lovers of God" has sprung into prominence in the last decade as never before. The multi-million-dollar contracts of athletes, the colossal arenas being constructed for sports events and the ever-increasing popularity of every kind of sport all testify to the timeliness of this prophecy. Like the Epicureans of old, men of today are committed to one god—the gratification of the flesh.

"Having a form of godliness but denying the power thereof." What can this mean? To this author the answer seems obvious. The form and ritual are all present, but the power of godliness is gone. What is the power of godliness? What makes a man godly? There is only one answer—the Gospel. I cannot help but believe that Paul was referring to the same thing of which he spoke in Romans 1:16 when he said, "I am not ashamed of the gospel of Christ: for it is the power of God unto salvation to every one that believeth." We live in a day when the "form of godliness" is present, but the power of it is gone. Huge edifices have been constructed in which to worship. Services are conducted according to strict form and ritual. Everything seems very "religious" and mystical. The tragedy is that the power of it all is gone!

The author once heard the late Dr. Charles E. Fuller say that he loved to go out into the country and preach in the small country churches, for there he could preach the Gospel and have Christian fellowship. He stated that the places where the Gospel is preached today are becoming fewer and fewer and farther and farther between. Surely we are in the last days of the "last days."

Paul's admonition concerning Timothy's attitude (and ours) toward such individuals is brief—"From such turn away."

II. THE SORT OF MEN DESCRIBED (vv. 6-9).

A. Their actions (vv. 6-7).

The men described in verses 1-5 are not without a religious bent as seen in verse 5. However, because they have only a "form of godliness"; and have never experienced the new birth, their lives manifest the sin which is in their hearts. Using religion as a pretense, they "creep into houses, and lead captive silly women laden with sins." The obvious reading of this verse implies sexual immorality. This is no doubt the primary inference. However, it may not be limited to this. These women who are laden down with sins, like the men who come to them, are open to a religion without repentance, salvation without the sacrifice of Christ, and forgiveness without the grace of God. How strange it is that people who are living in the grossest of sins will at the same time declare themselves to be very religious. The Greek word describing the women is literally "little women." It is a diminutive form of the word and in this case carries the meaning of contempt, hence "silly" women.

Because these women are carrying the burden of sin, they are "ever learning" from every religious quack and new idea that comes along, but they never find the truth. The author recalls a conversation of a few years ago with a woman who was a "lecturer" for one of the major cults of today. She had been married several times and was separated from her most recent husband. Her life was anything but exemplary and her religion matched it. She had a little bit of Scripture twisted with the philosophies of men, the result of which was a grand mess. Yet she was giving "lectures" to guide others. The "knowledge of the truth" comes by knowing Him who is "the way, the truth and the life" (John 14:6). This kind of knowledge comes by heart surrender to the Saviour, not by intellectual pursuits. Without this, the intellect is blind to spiritual truth, and no matter how one may study the religions or philosophies of the world, he will still be devoid of "the truth."

B. Their predecessors (v. 8).

The reference to Jannes and Jambres is probably the account of them resisting Moses at the time when he confronted Pharaoh to ask for the freedom of Israel. These may be some of the ones who performed miracles similar to those of Moses and thus caused Pharaoh to harden his heart. However, the illustration is not used because the men performed miracles, nor does it necessarily imply that they were surrounded with silly women laden with sins. The point is that just as these withstood Moses, so these false teachers resist the truth of God as presented by His true disciples. To this author it seems significant that today there is a great upsurge in interest in the miraculous, from certain "psychic" individuals to all forms of miracles claimed in connection with satanic worship. Could this be paving the way for the soon coming of the one who performs the "powers and signs and lying wonders"? Whether it be in Moses' day, our day, or that of the coming man of sin, all such miracles are from Satan himself and are directed toward that which has ever been the object of all satanic activity, opposition to the Truth of God.

"Withstood" and "resist" are the translations of the same Greek word meaning "to set oneself against." These are not men who have a slight misunderstanding of the truth but those who are dead set against it. Those who hear the truth and reject it become hardened in heart and come to oppose it. First, there is the inner urge to respond to the truth, then vacillation, then rejection, and ultimately opposition.

Such individuals are described as "utterly corrupted in mind." The term in Greek here is a perfect participle. The significance of the perfect tense is that it marks a point in time in which something was done with the result that it continues to the present time. These men heard the truth and rejected it. Their minds thus became corrupt. The final description of these false teachers is that they are "reprobate concerning the faith." The Greek word is *adokimos* which means to test by a standard and be disapproved. The men of this passage have been tested by the standard of the Christian faith and have been "disapproved."

C. Their destiny (v. 9).

These false teachers are headed for judgment and defeat. They may seem to triumph for a time and may gain many followers (as indicated in 2:16 and 3:13), but God will reveal them for what they are. The magicians of Moses' day might cause rods to become serpents, turn water to blood and cause frogs to come up out of a river, but the time came when they could go no farther. It is as if God were saying, "this far and no farther." So it will be with the false teachers. "Their folly [literally "senselessness"] shall be made manifest."

III. THE SAINT OF GOD IN CONTRAST (vv. 10-13).

A. Paul's life and suffering (vv. 10-11).

In great contrast to the false teachers just described, Paul points to nine characteristics of his own life that should challenge Timothy and be an example to anyone who was tempted to follow these false leaders. "The tree is known by its fruit," and the life of Paul spoke more loudly than anything that others might say.

"Thou hast fully known" is "to follow one so as to always be at his side," or "to join as a disciple." Timothy knew Paul's life more intimately than probably any other man knew it. He was Paul's son in the faith and had traveled with him. If there was a flaw in Paul's Christian life or if it failed to correspond to the doctrine he preached, Timothy should have known it. Blessed is the man who, like Paul, can say to his closest associates, "Look at my life. It is a demonstration of what I preach." His strong faith gave him purpose in life. The result was long-suffering, love and patience (or endurance).

Verse 11 shows the reaction of the world to such a life as Paul's—that of persecution and affliction. These words may seem to mean the same, but the first is harassment, thus resulting in suffering. Timothy is reminded of an early experience in his acquaintance with Paul, when on his first missionary journey Paul suffered great persecution at Antioch, Iconium and Lystra, even being stoned and left for dead at the last city. Timothy may not have been a Christian at this time, and the witness of Paul's suffering may have had much to do with his coming to Christ. Timothy's heart must have been touched when the old apostle testified of God's goodness by saying, "But out of them all the Lord delivered me." This is quite a statement in view of the fact that he was now in prison and knew that this time there was not likely to be deliverance from physical death. Although Paul was to face martyrdom, for him death would be only gain (Phil. 1:21) because it would mean immediate entrance into glory and the fellowship of his Lord.

B. Our lives and suffering (v. 12).

Nero was probably on the throne when Paul wrote these words. He did not say, "All who will live godly in Christ Jesus shall suffer persecution until Nero dies." Jesus warned that the world (men who are not born again) is at opposition with Him, and if we take our stand with Him the world will be against us, too (John 15:18-20). The same evil heart dwells in men today as did in the hearts of those who crucified the Saviour.

C. It won't get easier (v. 13).

What a contrast in this verse to the philosophy of the world today. The world says men and conditions are getting better and better. God says men and conditions will only get worse until He takes a hand in human history. The word "seduce" simply means "to lead astray." We usually use it in connection with moral seduction. This is certainly meant here, and it is true that this is true today as never before. Modern man today almost makes a career of moral seduction. However, we need to be reminded that there are other forms of seduction which are also increasing—intellectual seduction and spiritual seduction for example. Men are being led astray intellectually. The greatest example today is the satanic lie of communism. Millions are being led astray and into captivity by this lie. Perhaps the greatest area of seduction is that of the spirit. Men are being led astray spiritually as never before. This is the day of apostasy when men and churches are turning away from the preaching and teaching of the fundamental truths of the Word of God.

IV. THE SCRIPTURES—SUFFICIENT FOR ALL DAYS (vv. 14-16).

A. Persist in the Scriptures (vv. 14-15).

It was from a godly mother and grandmother that Timothy had learned the Scriptures. How important it is for Christian parents not only to teach the Word of God to their children but to help them to memorize it in their tender years. Fruit will be born of this during the entire lifetime.

Not only is the Word of God that which produces faith unto salvation, but after we become children of God it becomes our spiritual food. Therefore, we need to "continue" in it. There is no spiritual growth apart from the sacred Book. Read it. Memorize it. Meditate on it.

B. The origin and purpose of the Scriptures (vv. 16-17).

This is one of the great passages of the New Testament claiming that

God is the author of our Bible. The King James Version translation ("by inspiration") is not a strong presentation of the meaning of the Greek text. It literally says, "All Scripture is God-breathed." The very breath of God brought about the origin of Scripture. He led the Bible writers to write down the very words they wrote. Sometimes He told them what to write. Sometimes He chose just the men with just the personalities and just the vocabularies that when they wrote they were writing exactly what He wanted written, word for word. Sometimes they had knowledge that they were writing Scriptures. Sometimes they did not. However, back of it all was the sovereign hand of God guiding the hand of the human authors. This is true of *all* Scripture.

It also says that *"all* scripture . . . is profitable." God led not only in inspiration but in preservation, and even the portions of the Word from which we may not seem to "get a blessing" are profitable to us if we devote time to their study. God has given us His complete revelation that the man of God may be "perfect." This does not mean sinless perfection, but "complete." God has given us in His Word all that we need to equip us for the life to which He has called us. If we will only study the Bible, He will see to it that we are "throughly furnished [literally: completely fitted out] unto all good works." Therefore, let us give a portion of time each day to the diligent study of God's textbook for our lives.

Questions for discussion:

1. What evidences do you see today of conditions described in the first five verses of this chapter?

2. How do you evaluate the flourishing of cults today in the light of Paul's statement that false teachers shall proceed no further?

3. What forms do persecutions take today?

4. Why do you think that the inspiration of the Scriptures is so strongly attacked by religious liberals and unbelievers?

13

Last but Not Least

II Timothy 4:1-22

THE CHAPTER OUTLINED:

I. The Final Charge to Timothy

II. The Final Warning of Apostasy

III. The Final Testimony of a Faithful Servant

IV. The Final Account of Friends and Foes

V. The Final Words of Paul

As we enter the portals of this last chapter of II Timothy, we do so quietly and reverently because this is hallowed ground. We are about to read the last words ever written by the great apostle Paul. He knew his martyrdom was not far distant, and he wrote with this in mind. There is sadness in our hearts because we have come to love this great man of God, and yet we are filled with joy and praise to God because we know that his sufferings are nearly over and nothing but glory lies ahead. Let us listen very carefully to his final admonitions to Timothy (and thus to us).

I. THE FINAL CHARGE TO TIMOTHY (vv. 1-2, 5).

If the author has counted correctly, this is the fourth charge that is given to Timothy in the two epistles. The others are in I Timothy 1:18; 5:21 and 6:13. Although two different Greek words are used, they are both properly translated "charge." The significance of the one used in this passage is that what he is about to say is being solemnly testified before God. It is not merely good advice but something to which Paul is bearing witness "through and through." It could also be translated "adjure." These final words are important and not to be taken lightly.

This charge is given in the presence of "God and our Lord Jesus Christ." Paul recognized that these words were spoken in the presence of Deity, and he wanted Timothy to realize this, too. Wuest says that the particular construction of the words here calls for a translation which should be read "God, even Christ Jesus" ("Lord" is not in the best Greek texts). This would mean that Paul is referring to Jesus Christ as God. Although this may be the proper translation, it cannot be said to be the exclusive meaning. However, had Paul considered our Lord less than God, he should not have used these words. This is another of the many instances in which so far as Paul was concerned our Lord Jesus Christ is equated with the God of heaven.

This charge is also given in the light of the fact that the judgment of all men lies ahead. Our Lord Jesus Christ will judge "the quick and the dead at his appearing and his kingdom." The word "quick" has changed in its meaning since the King James Version was translated. Today it means "fast" or "sudden." In that day it meant "alive" which is the meaning here. The terms "the quick and the dead" may refer to those who are physically alive and those dead at the time of the second coming of Christ. However, this author feels that Paul is speaking of two different groups of people—the saved and the lost. The word "quick" is used frequently in the

New Testament to speak of those who have spiritual life (John 5:21; 6:63; Eph. 2:5; Col. 2:13). It comes from the Greek word *zao* meaning "to live or to be alive." While this may refer to physical life and is so used in the New Testament, it also speaks of the spiritual life which is given by the new birth. Those who are alive or the "quick" in this passage seem to be set in contrast with "the dead." This last term cannot help but remind us of the scene in Revelation 20:11-15 where unsaved men stand before God for final judgment and sentence. Four times these are spoken of as "the dead."

The time of judgment is spoken of as "at his appearing and his kingdom." Although the author has found no other commentator who so interprets the passage, and thus I will not be dogmatic about it, I am made to wonder if this does not refer to the Judgment Seat of Christ for the Christian and the Great White Throne Judgment for the unsaved. The word "appear" is used to speak of that time when Christ shall come for His own (cf. I Peter 1:7 and II Tim. 4:6). This is to be followed by the Judgment Seat of Christ where the works of the Christian are to undergo the fire of God's judgment (I Cor. 3:11-15). This will be the time of the judgment of those who have been "quickened" or made alive in Christ by the Holy Spirit. In contrast is the Great White Throne Judgment of "the dead" or unsaved which comes immediately at the close of our Lord's kingdom reign here on earth (see Rev. 20). Thus the "quick" will be judged "at his appearing" and "the dead" at "his kingdom." Whether this be that which the Holy Spirit intended to teach in this passage or not, one thing is clear—men will be judged, and Paul was giving this solemn charge to Timothy in the light of that fact.

What was the charge? What was Paul's last commission to this one who would carry on his ministry? Preach the Word! It cannot be overemphasized or said strongly enough that Paul had only one message—the Word of God. It is interestning and important to note that Paul spoke of this in the first chapter of the first book he ever wrote and in the last chapter of the last book he wrote. In I Thessalonians 1:5 and 8 he spoke of "the gospel" which he had proclaimed to the Thessalonians and "the word of the Lord" which through them had been preached to all that area.

We are to be at this business of proclaiming God's Word all the time. Someone has said that instead of four seasons, Paul knew only two—"in" and "out." We are to preach the Gospel and teach the Word of God when it is convenient and when it is not convenient, when we feel like it and when we don't feel like it, when the audience is favorable or when it is unfavorable. Be diligent all the time!

The next few words tell of some of the hardest tasks a pastor ever has to perform. It is not hard to commend and give words of praise for spiritual growth or faithfulness (which we also ought to be careful to do!), but for the undershepherd to have to go to one of the sheep to "reprove, rebuke, exhort" is so very difficult. Most pastors would rather dig ditches for eight hours than spend an hour in such ministry. It hurts to lovingly rebuke people. Yet let me emphasize, fellow pastor, that we had better be sure to do it when it needs to be done! Hours of difficulty and further problems may be avoided if we will only heed these words. Dr. Bob Jones, Sr., used to say, "The way to avoid trouble is by having trouble." Let us remember, however, that only "longsuffering and doctrine" will be used of the Holy Spirit to bring submission and correction in the life of the one to whom we must speak.

The charge continues in verse 5 with the admonition to "watch thou in all things." The term has its basis in being sober in relation to drink. Just as a man is not to be intoxicated and thus lose control of himself, so Timothy was to keep alert for deviation from spiritual truth and proper conduct in the Lord's work and among His people. "Do the work of an evangelist" are words that ought to be on a plaque on every preacher's desk. The evangelist is one whose primary responsibility and calling is the spreading of the Gospel. The pastor may have many demands upon his time and many other responsibilities to fulfill, but he is first and foremost a child of God who, like all other Christians, is called to be a winner of souls.

He is also challenged to "make full proof" of his ministry. This means to carry out to the end or to perform completely. A few verses later Paul is going to claim that he has done so (v. 7), and he wants Timothy to do the same. Every individual who has undertaken to serve the Lord in any way would do well to read carefully and heed the charge given in these verses.

II. THE FINAL WARNING OF APOSTASY (vv. 3-4).

The words of these verses have never been more appropriate than today. Paul spoke of conditions when "the time will come when they will not endure sound doctrine." If that time is not now, I would dread to be here when it comes! The word "endure" means "to hold oneself upright or firm against a person or thing." This is the attitude of the modern-day liberal theologian toward the sound doctrine of the Word of God.

We should note that the "they" of verse 3 refers not to the preachers in the pulpit but the people in the pews! The reason there are so many liberal, unbelieving preachers in the pulpits of America today is because there are liberal, unbelieving people before them who want that kind of preaching and will stand for no other! The infidelity of modernism would never have gained a foothold in this country if the so-called church people would have demanded sound doctrine. However, when unbelieving, unsaved preachers began to stand in pulpits and deny the truths of the Word of God, it was just what the unregenerated hearts of audiences wanted to hear. The audiences "heaped to themselves" preachers and teachers that would give their "itching" ears exactly what they wanted to hear and "scratch them" where they wanted to be scratched.

Verse 4 is very important. Note that first these people "turn away" from the truth and then they are "turned" to fables. The first is active, the second is passive. When men deliberately turn from the truth of God they lay themselves open to every deceit of the devil. The author just recently listened to Dr. Merrill Unger, who has written much on demonology, speak on that subject. Of all that he said, nothing was emphasized more strongly than that when an individual resists or rejects the Spirit of God, he thus lays himself open to a deceiving spirit. There may be far more of this in the world today than most of us recognize.

III. THE FINAL TESTIMONY OF A FAITHFUL SERVANT (vv. 6-8).

This is one of the greatest testimonies of a servant of God in the Bible and some of the most precious words of Scripture. Oh, that I, as well as every child of God, could give similar testimony when I come to the end of my earthly journey.

Paul had given everything he had to Jesus Christ. He now was ready to offer all that was left—his physical life. This is the meaning of "I am now ready to be offered." The Greek speaks of the pouring out of a drink-offering before God. Paul was ready to pour out his physical life as his last offering to the Lord he loved. The term "my departure" speaks of a soldier striking his tent to go home, a ship lifting anchor to sail away, or the removing of shackles from a prisoner for his release. All of the metaphors aptly describe Paul's coming death. It was not something of which he was to be a victim. It was a release, a going home.

The three "I haves" of verse 7 speak of a life of utter faithfulness. Paul fought, when necessary, against those who would stand against his Lord.

He faithfully completed the calling which God had given him, and he had "kept by guarding" (literal meaning) the faith which had been committed to him. That doctrine which he had admonished Timothy to guard carefully and against which false teachers would come, Paul had faithfully guarded and kept himself.

"Henceforth!" No, suffering and martyrdom were not the end for Paul. They were only the beginning. There is a "henceforth" for every child of God as he nears the end of life's road. You can almost sense the excitement in Paul and the joy of his words as he states the remainder of the verse. The "crown" spoken of here is one of the many crowns of rewards to be given to the faithful child of God, and this is one that all may have, for it is given to all who "love his appearing."

IV. THE FINAL ACCOUNT OF FRIENDS AND FOES
(vv. 9-18).

This is an intensely human section. Paul was not some superhuman person who was not affected by physical problems or hurt when others turned against him. He was just an ordinary man with an above-ordinary dedication to Jesus Christ.

Twice in this chapter (vv. 9 and 21) Paul asked Timothy to come to him as soon as possible. Paul was alone, and he needed the strength that Timothy's companionship could provide. We who serve the Lord today need to remember these words. Paul was strengthened by the Lord as perhaps few of us have been, and yet he felt the need of Christian companionship in this hour of trial. Believers today need to be conscious of brothers and sisters in Christ who need our help and comfort in their hour of need.

In verses 10-12 a list of Paul's fellow laborers and their present activity is given. It must have hurt Paul deeply to have to write concerning Demas. He had been with Paul at Rome during his first imprisonment (Col. 4:14; Philemon 24) but now had departed to Thessalonica. Some feel that although Demas had forsaken Paul, he may not have turned away from Christ but had returned to Thessalonica which may have been his home since he is mentioned in Philemon 24 with Aristarchus, a Thessalonian. However, he is spoken of as "having loved this present world (literally: "age"). This would indicate that he at least had buckled under the pressure of persecution in Rome and forsook the aged apostle.

Crescens, Titus and Tychicus had evidently been dispatched by the apostle Paul on special missions to the places mentioned even though it does not specifically state this concerning the first two. No doubt Paul would have desired that these remain with him during his suffering. But as when Paul had sent Timothy to Thessalonica during his earlier ministry (I Thess. 3:1-2), the work of the Lord came first no matter what personal sacrifice might be involved.

Dr. Luke was the only one with Paul. This says a lot about Luke. He evidently chose to remain with him in spite of the danger to his personal safety. Luke was the one to whom Paul dictated several of his letters and was no doubt writing the final lines for the great apostle.

A rather touching note is heard in the last part of verse 11. Paul asks for Mark to be brought to him. You will recall that Mark is the one who forsook Paul and Barnabas on the first missionary journey. He has caused a division between the two missionary leaders when Barnabas wanted to take him along on the second journey, but Paul refused. This caused Paul and Barnabas to go their separate ways, and all sorts of speculation has been made as to who was right in the matter. Anyway, as often happens in disputes, perhaps both men had now mellowed and changed in their attitude. Mark evidently had given his life anew to the Lord and had proved himself a worthy servant of the Master. Paul would not have requested his coming or have stated that he was profitable for the ministry if this had not been true. On the other hand, perhaps Paul had grown in grace and tenderness since that first rejection of Mark. Now the one who was rejected by Paul for unfaithfulness was to have a special place of ministry in the life of this one who was about to suffer martyrdom.

Because of the cold and dampness of the dungeon in which he was imprisoned, Paul asked Timothy to bring his cloak. This was a kind of circular cape of very heavy material which would not be needed in summer but was much needed now, especially with winter ahead. He also requested "books" and the "parchments." Paul's request for these says much about the discipline and study of this man of God. Although he anticipated that martyrdom was not far ahead, he continued the intense study which had characterized his life. This ought to be a rebuke to many preachers and teachers of the Word of God who do not spend the time they should in the study of the Word of God before preaching or teaching. To be an expositor of the Bible requires time and hard study—Spirit-filled study, yes, but plain, hard, diligent study.

Alexander, the coppersmith (literally: metal-worker), is not clearly identified. Since there were many Alexanders in those days, he cannot be specified as the one mentioned in I Timothy 1:20. Neither can we be certain that he was one of those who arose against Paul during the uproar at Ephesus concerning the goddess Diana (Acts 19), although this seems more likely since Timothy was at Ephesus when Paul was writing and metal working was a leading industry in this city of idol worshipers. Paul recognizes the fact that Alexander's evil deeds will not go unpunished. The Greek shows that Paul was not expressing a wish or his own desire in the punishment of Alexander. The apostle was not vindictive. He simply stated that God would someday mete out judgment on Alexander because of the evil deeds that he had done. Paul also warns Timothy against this man and the evil that he may yet do.

His trial at Rome is now spoken of by Paul. The word "answer" is a technical word referring to a verbal defense in a judicial trial. It literally means "to talk one's self off from." The idea is to verbally talk a person from off the charge against him. "No man stood with me" refers to one who could have legally substantiated his claims. Perhaps this was some influential person in Rome who could have aided in his defense. It may have been that the persecution was so intense that there was no Christian who would come to his side. We may wonder where Luke was at this time, but it is possible that he had not yet arrived in Rome when the first defense took place.

Paul was alone, yet not alone. The One who is always faithful stood by him. Not only did the Lord strengthen him to present his defense but he was emboldened to give the Gospel to all that official group who heard him speak. Nero, himself, may have presided at this trial, and it is possible that this tyrant of a ruler heard the gospel of God's grace and forgiveness from the apostle Paul's own lips.

What is meant by "delivered from the mouth of the lion" is not clear. Since Paul was a Roman citizen he would not be fed to the lions. Some have thought this to be a reference to Nero. It may also mean the dire circumstances of the moment with which Paul was faced. Whatever it meant, Paul had the confidence that God would continue to deliver him. He knew that his life was in the hands of his Lord and nothing could touch him unless it first passed through the hands of a sovereign God, his loving Heavenly Father. What faith! What confidence in an hour of supreme trial. He knew he was going to be kept by God, and by whatever means he might face death, nothing could rob him of fellowship with his Lord in the kingdom above. In the midst of his present suffering and future death, this called for a doxology from the great heart of this choice servant of God.

V. THE FINAL WORDS OF PAUL (vv. 19-22).

Although personal matters bore heavily upon him, Paul did not forget kind greetings to friends in Ephesus. He recounts the whereabouts of friends that Timothy would know. The fact that Trophimus was left at Miletum sick shows that although Paul had the apostolic gift of healing (Acts 28:8), he recognized that it was not always God's will to heal.

A list of friends at Rome, known to Paul and Timothy, is given as sending greetings. Evidently these had seen Paul recently but were not with him now (v. 11). Paul, however, knew that they would want to be remembered to Timothy.

Paul concludes with a benediction that our Lord Jesus Christ might be with Timothy and that he might experience His grace. He could have desired nothing greater for his son in the faith. To have the realization that the One who said, "Lo, I am with you alway, even unto the end of the world [age]" is with us in the greatest need of the child of God as we seek to do His will here below. With His presence every grace will be supplied that we need to face whatever may come in the path of His will for our lives. Without Him, life is less than useless. With Him, a dungeon can be a sanctuary of glory.

Although the author has used the word "final" to outline the writing of Paul in this chapter (final charge, final apostasy, final testimony, and so forth), in no sense does this mean a sense of finality for the great apostle. The last chapter of this book is being written during the month of May when many seniors are looking forward to "commencement" exercises. There is always a sense of finality at such a program, but it is correctly named—it is a commencement. It is a graduation from a time of training and preparation to commence the task toward which the preparation is made. Thus the apostle Paul was about to experience his "graduation" day. He was about to commence that glorious eternity of reward and fellowship with his Saviour for which God's grace has been preparing him. May the writer and reader of these lines so dedicate our lives to our blessed Lord that we, too, shall have an abundant entrance into His presence.

Questions for discussion:

1. How may the average person determine whether or not a minister is following Paul's admonition to "preach the word"? What should we look for?

2. In what ways may verse 5 be applied to every Christian as to those

who serve in the pastorate or other special ministry?

3. In addition to the "crown of righteousness," what other crowns can you name that are mentioned in the New Testament and for what are they to be given?

4. What are some of the ways that God may use to deliver the Christian from "every evil work" (v. 18)?

Bibliography

Barnes, Albert. *Notes on the New Testament.* Grand Rapids, Michigan: Baker Book House, 1963.

Harrison, Everett F. *Introduction to the New Testament.* Grand Rapids, Michigan: Wm. B. Eerdmans Publishing Company, 1971.

Hendriksen, William. "Exposition of the Pastoral Epistles," *New Testament Commentary.* Grand Rapids, Michigan: Baker Book House, 1957.

Kent, Jr., Homer A. *The Pastoral Epistles.* Unpublished notes for class in English Bible at Grace Theological Seminary, Winona Lake, Indiana, 1954.

————, *The Pastoral Epistles.* Chicago: Moody Press, 1958.

King, Guy H. *A Leader Led.* Fort Washington, Pennsylvania: Christian Literature Crusade, 1951.

————, *To My Son.* Fort Washington, Pennsylvania: Christian Literature Crusade, 1944.

Lenski, R. C. H. *The Interpretation of St. Paul's Epistles to the Thessalonians, to Timothy, to Titus and to Philemon.* Minneapolis, Minnesota: Augsburg Publishing House, 1937.

Robertson, A. T. *Word Pictures in the New Testament.* Nashville, Tennessee: Broadman Press, 1930.

Vine, W. E. *An Expository Dictionary of New Testament Words.* Westwood, New Jersey: Fleming H. Revell Company, 1940.

Wuest, Kenneth S. *The Pastoral Epistles in the Greek New Testament.* Grand Rapids, Michigan: Wm. B. Eerdmans Publishing Company, 1952.